CRYSTAL BEACH
Out of the Park

Gary Pooler

◆ **FriesenPress**

One Printers Way
Altona, MB R0G 0B0
Canada

www.friesenpress.com

Copyright © 2022 by Gary Pooler
First Edition — 2021

Cover photo credits:
Comet: Dale Roddick.
Phil Edwards: Canadian Sports Hall of Fame.
John Heenan: Library of Congress.
Constable Badge: Mark Chernish.

Some material and photographs in this book are older than 100 years and are part of the public domain. I have still credited any and all sources whether in the public domain or not. If a photo or image in this book is your intellectual or personal property, and I am misusing or misrepresenting it in anyway, please contact me with verification of ownership with either a copyright or trademark certificate, and I will re-cite or remove it upon request. Request must be made to the author by the owner of the property or legal representative of the owner only.

All rights reserved.

No part of this publication may be reproduced in any form, or by any means, electronic or mechanical, including photocopying, recording, or any information browsing, storage, or retrieval system, without permission in writing from FriesenPress.

ISBN
978-1-03-913024-1 (Hardcover)
978-1-03-913023-4 (Paperback)
978-1-03-913025-8 (eBook)

1. HISTORY, NORTH AMERICA

Distributed to the trade by The Ingram Book Company

Table of Contents

Introduction v
Foreword: Religion or Recreation? vii
Chapter One: Circus by the Sea 1
Chapter Two: The Prize Fighters 73
Chapter Three: The Saugerties Bard 85
Chapter Four: Crystal Beach Stadium 95
Chapter Five: Law and Disorder 125
Chapter Six: Michael John O'Leary, V.C. 167
Chapter Seven: The Vaudevillians 183
Chapter Eight: The Circus Leaves Town 195
About the Author 207
Reeves of Crystal Beach 209
Police Chiefs of Crystal Beach 211
Fire Chiefs of Crystal Beach 213
Sons of Crystal Beach who died in service of our country: 215
130 Years of Crystal Beach Cottage Names 217
Acknowledgements 223
Sources 225

INTRODUCTION

This book came to life while researching the lives of two retired vaudeville performers who had settled in the village of Crystal Beach, Ontario in 1929. The village was famous for the Crystal Beach Amusement Park, which existed for over one hundred years on the northeast shore of Lake Erie. During my research, many fascinating and unheard-of stories from within the village and surrounding area kept popping up. Stories that may or may not have made the press at the time, but were forgotten, perhaps by choice, by historians and many residents of the village. Unusual, offbeat stories with little or no amusement park connection. Some locals may be familiar with them, but these tales will also appeal to the millions of people who visited the amusement park, and to newcomers to Crystal Beach. Hopefully, people will read about this unique place and its history and want to experience the "Beach" vibe themselves. Until now, these stories have never been written down. Many more Crystal Beach stories simply cannot, nor ever will, be told in a book.

Throughout the book, the general area will be referred to simply as "the Beach," the village's nickname used by locals for decades.

In addition to the village's police, political, and bootlegging scandals, many other intriguing events occurred in and around Crystal Beach, and many famous people attended them. These stories are being lost to history. Local politics, bare-knuckle boxing, track and field, bootlegging, and murder are not usually covered in a Crystal Beach history book. But they are becoming a lost part of our village's history. The main character in this book is the village itself.

Chapter One, "Circus by the Sea," is in three parts and paints an overall picture of the amusement park and the atmosphere it created within and around the village for one-hundred-plus years. The remaining chapters take place, as the title implies, "out of the park." Every generation, the Roaring Twenties, the big band era, right up to the late 80s, will each have their own special recollections of Crystal Beach, just as a child from the 60s will. While the amusement park created timeless memories for millions of visitors, the village did the same for the people who lived and raised families there, and who called it home.

The research for this book is based on historical media reports, academic papers, books, on-line articles, and police reports, woven into a narrative format. Personal experience from having grown up in Crystal Beach, interviews with longtime residents, and oral history also comprise source material. My interpretations of the evidence gathered are made in good faith. Legend and folklore are referred to as such.

Bear in mind that this is not a pictorial book. Many of the old, grainy photographs are included simply for visual reference in describing certain places, events, and people from decades ago. Most can be seen in better resolution at crystalbeachoutofthepark.ca or at Crystal Beach: Out of the Park on Facebook.

Gary Pooler

FOREWORD:
RELIGION OR RECREATION?

It has long been generally assumed that Crystal Beach began as a religious "colony" or "campground." Some believe it started out purely as a recreational resort. However, it is not a simple either/or scenario.

1887: John E. Rebstock acquired the Bertie Township property. After a failed attempt at sand-mining, Rebstock originally *intended* to start a religious camp, but this idea was almost immediately "hijacked" by other non-religious activities. There would be no formal or chartered religious camp established until 1895.

1888: Being a devoutly religious Methodist, Rebstock based his idea for a Chautauqua-style camp meeting in Crystal Beach on similar ones that he had seen in Cottage City, Massachusetts. He advertised it as a picnic area and campground, while also encouraging spiritual and educational activities in the grove area. He invited guest lecturers. Visitors camped in tents and rustic cottages while lectures and sermons simultaneously took place within the grove. They enjoyed the swings, water slides, concessions, amusements, and side shows growing along a primitive midway. Religion and entertainment managed to co-exist for only a year or two. There was no "colony", nor any religious "camp meeting" organization in Crystal Beach at this point. There were few, if any, winter residents at all.

In 1889, Mr. Rebstock accepted that the campers preferred amusements and concessions over religious activities. Spiritual and intellectual sermons in the woods were still sporadically held, but they were losing popularity and attendees.

In 1890, Rebstock announced that the resort would be re-imagined solely as an amusement park and picnic grounds, known as Crystal Beach Amusement Park.

In 1895, the first officially chartered Chautauqua-style camp meeting was established in Crystal Beach. Opening day for the Crystal Beach International Assembly was on July 1, 1895, eight years after John E. acquired the property.

In 1896, the C.B.I.A. conducted its second, and final season. Religious services continued nomadically and were conducted wherever the various "assemblies" could gather: at the assembly grounds, the Assembly House, the amphitheatre, in tents, and also at the roller rink within the park. Contrary to popular belief, Queens Circle never became the centre of worship. The Chautauqua idea simply never caught on, and the Crystal Beach International Assembly ceased to exist.

CHAPTER ONE:
CIRCUS BY THE SEA

THE BEGINNING

There are numerous historical works and pictorial reviews about the famous Crystal Beach Amusement Park. They offer many perspectives and memories of fun and youthful times at the park and on the beach. A book about growing up and living in Crystal Beach would be incomplete without at least an overview of the park, and how it permeated life in the village. Strange events and eccentric people somehow seem all the more intriguing when they take place against the backdrop of a carnival-like beach town.

In the late 1880s, an American entrepreneur named John Evangelist Rebstock began transforming 150 acres of barren farmland in Bertie Township, Ontario into a village, a carnival, and a community, creating a hometown for generations and heartfelt memories for millions.

John E. Rebstock, (or John E., as he will periodically be referred to) was born in 1852 in Buffalo, New York, to John Rebstock and Catherine Klepser. Although the name is rooted in German, John E.'s middle son George J. Rebstock, wrote in his booklet that his father's parents were immigrants from the Alsace-Loraine region of France. This is confusing, as that region and name weren't created until 1871, well after the Rebstocks had emigrated to America. At the time of their residence there, it would have still been part of Germany.

After settling in the Black Rock section of Buffalo, the family first moved to Bertie Township in the late 1850s and lived on the south side of Nigh Road, just west of Gorham. The property owner's name at that time is shown on the 1862 Tremaine's map as J. E. Rebstock, father and son likely having the same initials, as John E. would have only been ten years old at that time.

While living on Nigh Road, J. E.'s siblings were Mary, Emma, Joseph, Rachel, and Albert. Two other brothers, George and Stephen, remained in Buffalo. After the U.S. Civil War ended, the Rebstocks moved back to Buffalo, but John E. returned to Bertie Township on his own as a young man. In addition to other jobs, he worked on the Barnhart farm in Bertie Township for forty dollars for the entire summer.

John E. Rebstock, founder of Crystal Beach, circa 1890.

Photo: Courtesy Cheryl Fretz Carlyle

One of his chores with Mr. Barnhart was hauling logs down Ridge Road (now Ridgeway Road) to the lakeshore. The logs had to go either over, or through, the dunes in order to float them over the lake to Buffalo for use in construction. He would have become very familiar with the Bertie Township lakefront area and the dunes, even this early in his life.

John E. again returned to Buffalo and worked in the real estate business, and owned a stove company on Washington Street. He was deeply involved in Black Rock and Riverside area business, real estate, religious, and political activities. He married Alice Mason from Vermont, and they had seven children together: Louise, Walter, Arthur, George J., Ralph, Carl, and Thelma. Alice Rebstock died in 1914, and John re-married to Mamie Todd.

Historical records indicate that in 1887, John E. acquired the land where Crystal Beach would come to be. For historical perspective, six years earlier in Tombstone, Arizona, Wyatt Earp, two of his brothers, and their friend Doc Holliday, killed three cowboys in a gun fight at the O.K. Corral. Just five years earlier, Jesse James had been shot and killed by Robert Ford in Missouri.

Family history from his son George J. Rebstock indicates that John E. acquired the farmland from a Mr. Morris. The initial property acquisition by Rebstock was 150 acres on Lot 25, Broken Front Concession, Bertie Township, which extended from Ridge Road westward to the Herbert Haun farm at Elmwood. Tremaine's map shows that in 1862 Lot 25 was owned by Mathias Haun, who then sold the 150-acre parcel in 1865 to Edward Morris for $5,000. The Hauns had originally acquired the property from Ambrose Morningstar in 1836.[1]

John E. would subsequently acquire sections of several neighbouring farms, including portions of the Schooley farm to the west, and the Brackbill farm to the east. The initial Rebstock property, Lot 25, described later as "a barren wasteland" by John E., included from where Michener Road is today southward to the lakeshore, including the dunes and the beautiful sand beach.

Many historic accounts paint the romantic image of John E. Rebstock "discovering" Crystal Beach in 1887, and subsequently purchasing it to build a religious retreat. Although somewhat true, this is an over-simplification of the story.

The Rebstocks had previously lived in Bertie Township on Nigh Road in the late 1850s until after the Civil War, when they moved back to Buffalo. There is little doubt that John E. had extensive previous knowledge of the Haun/Morris property and surrounding area prior to 1887. In addition to having hauled logs either over or through the dunes as a young man, John E. had probably explored and played in the woods and bluffs along the lakeshore many times as a young boy when he and his family first lived in Bertie Township. One thing is certain: John E. Rebstock's first view of Abino Bay and the Crystal Beach shoreline happened sometime in the late 1850s, and was from the north, while playing atop one of the giant dunes, not in 1887 from a steamship out on the lake.

As the Rebstock property sloped down towards the lake from the glacial ridge known geologically as the Crystal Beach Moraine, it levelled off just before a large wooded grove, which is what it would come to be called for more than one hundred years. Although the ground immediately north of the dune in Crystal Beach had some marshy spots, because of the moraine's closer proximity to the shoreline on the Rebstock property, it was not nearly as wet as the Bay Beach and Point Abino areas further to the west.

There was no view of the lake from the grove in the early days, because in between it and the beach was a ninety-foot sand dune stretching along the entire shoreline. The bluff acted like a giant wind break against the breezes off of Lake Erie. After climbing up the north side of the dune and laying one's eyes upon Abino Bay from ninety feet above for the first time, with the wind blowing in off of the bay, it was undoubtedly a breathtaking sight, as it still is today.

Descending down the south side of the dune, one alit onto a beautiful white sandy beach, stretching for two miles around the sweeping curve of the Abino Bay. Rebstock knew that both the beach and the grove were places that people would flock to. When the idea to build a resort in that very spot came to him, he must have known immediately that he had hit the jackpot.

Envisioning people arriving by boat from Buffalo, Rebstock imagined a large passageway through the sand dune covered with wooden planks to allow for foot passage into the grove area. He could not possibly expect his guests to climb up and over the dune just to get to the grove. Eventually a large strip of sand was removed, and this pathway was referred to as the "cut". A formal wooden walkway and retaining walls were later built through the cut. This actually served two purposes: to allow foot passage from the boat landing to the grove, and also for the sand from the cut to be used as fill for some of the wetter areas north of the dune. The grove was a large wooded area, stretching from Ridge Road westward to where Ashwood Avenue and Schooley Road would later be. There was no Erie Road yet. This was the original gathering area in Crystal Beach.

John E. and his large family settled on the south side of what would eventually become Rebstock Road, between Derby and Elmwood, across from where Crystal Beach Public School would one day be built. This area would later come to be called Crystal Heights. At the time, there were no other houses between the Rebstock house and the lake. Other farms along the same road at the same time were the various Claus families of Jacob, Fred, Henry, Charles and Daniel. There were also the Brackbills, east of Ridge where, at that time, Rebstock Road was actually named Brackbill. On the west end of Rebstock Road, there was the Web and Herbert Haun farm, in addition to the Schooleys at the far west end.

The shoreline upon which the southern end of the Rebstock property lay was very serene and peaceful. Protected from the prevailing west winds by Point Abino, a large spit of sand jutting out into Lake Erie across Abino Bay from Crystal Beach. Large waves and undertows were unheard of in the calm waters of Abino Bay.

John E. Rebstock's home today on Rebstock Road.

Photo: Author

Initially, John E. and his family lived at the farm only during the summer months, going back to Buffalo for the winter. In 1898, the family moved to the Bertie Township farm year-round, and in 1910 the Rebstocks, with their two youngest children Carl and Thelma, started wintering in Florida.[2]

Oral family history handed down is that once the Ford Model T came out, John E. acquired one and he would drive his family to Florida and back each winter along early roads that were nothing more than dirt ruts. Their trip would take two to three weeks one-way, including several complete tire changes.[3] It was during one of these trips in 1912 that John E. and a Canadian business partner, Mr. Avery, renamed Seaside, Florida "Crystal Beach." Their intention was to build a winter resort for northerners.

The story of how Crystal Beach got its name has several debated versions. One is that John Rebstock chose the name either for the way the sun sparkled like crystals off the water in the bay, or for the look and texture of the crystalline white sand. John E. had initially hoped to export sand to Buffalo for construction through his newly-formed Lake Erie Sand Company. History reveals that Rebstock found much greater success with the resort business than with the sand company, which never actually began operations.

Another version is that in 1890, Rebstock chose the name after suggestions from a group of his Buffalo business associates, including the Mayor of Buffalo, Erastus C. Knight. In 1890, Knight was indeed a business partner of Rebstock but was not, in fact, the Mayor of Buffalo. He was still a real estate developer and investor at the time, and would not become Buffalo mayor until 1902, serving until 1905.

Pre-dating all the commonly-held historical accounts of the coining of the name "Crystal Beach" is a news article from the *Buffalo Morning Express* on July 2, 1887. The article reveals that in 1887, John Rebstock was not the only Buffalo businessman interested in the sand across the lake, or in the name "Crystal Beach." The Express article reports that Charles O. Rano, a Buffalo alderman and resident of Black Rock, announced his purchase of sixty acres of land on Point Abino from E.O. Page for $14,000. Rano announced that he was starting a sand company on Point Abino, and that he would call the place "Crystal Beach." Eerily similar, yet much prior to John E. Rebstock's plans for his own Crystal Beach on the other side of Abino Bay.

THE BUFFALO EXPRESS, SATURDAY MORNING, JULY 2, 1887.

C. O. Rano will soon go into the sand business. He has bought of E. O. Page 60 acres of land on the Canada shore, above Point Abino. The Alderman calls the place, for which he paid $14,000, Crystal Beach. The sand will be brought to this city in three scows by a tug.

Source: *Buffalo Morning Express*, 2 July 1887

The entire shoreline area surrounding the point and Abino Bay had been generally referred to as "Point Abino" since the 1700s, even though the name refers to the actual spit itself.

However, the property that Charles Rano purchased was literally right on the point, as the Page and Holloway families had held ownership of that land for years, and it was E.O. Page who sold the sixty acres to Rano. The name Crystal Beach, in reference to the general Point Abino area, had never been reported on or mentioned prior to Rano's announcement.

The backstory of Rano and Rebstock is very intriguing. John E. Rebstock and Charles Rano were both from the Riverside and Black Rock areas of Buffalo, New York. They were both very involved in local politics, real estate, and business. Although Rano was a chemist by profession, he was also a real estate investor, and an inventor. Like Rebstock, he owned a stove company, the Buffalo Stove Company. Charles Rano was also an elected official for the City of Buffalo, serving at various times as an alderman in both the 12th and 25th Wards.

Rebstock and Rano may have been rivals or they may possibly have been partners in certain ventures. However, since Rebstock owned the Rebstock Stove Company, and Rano owned the Buffalo Stove Company, it is more than likely that they were business competitors.

One of Rebstock's business partners, the aforementioned Buffalo real estate developer Erastus C. Knight, was also involved in Buffalo city politics at the time. Others in the group included Erie County Sherriff Arthur Jenkins, and Buffalo Attorney Arthur Hickman. There is little doubt that these gentlemen were aware of what Charles Rano was up to across the lake.

One thing is certain: When the *Buffalo Morning Express* came out on July 2, 1887 with the news of Councilman Rano's plans in Point Abino, Knight, Rebstock, and their circle of movers and shakers took notice. It appears that Rano and Rebstock may have been competing not only in the "hot stove league" in Buffalo, but were also racing towards the same potential prize across the water in Canada.

History tells us that Rebstock turned out to be the victor. Charles Rano subsequently appears nowhere as one of the initial group of investors in the Crystal Beach resort, and his proposed Point Abino sand operation never took on the name Crystal Beach.

Rebstock acquired his Bertie Township shoreline property around the same time that Rano's announcement appeared. Whether Rano cut a deal with the Rebstock and Knight group for the name, or whether he just got squeezed out, John E. and his Buffalo associates made their first announcement using the name Crystal Beach well after Rano's media release in 1887.

Perhaps he liked Rano's idea, and decided to mine sand on his own lakefront property. When that didn't work out, Rebstock then consulted with his Buffalo business partners about changing direction. This group's "Crystal Beach" would be on the east side of Abino Bay, not out on the Point. The inside story of what actually happened between the two business rivals and their dealings around Abino Bay will never fully be known, but it would be a fascinating tale indeed.

While it can be accurately stated that the Rebstock-Knight group out of Buffalo definitely founded the Crystal Beach that we know today, they were not the first to attempt to use the actual name on the Canadian side of the lake.

In regards to the discussion of whether Crystal Beach started as a religious colony or as a business venture, it is significant to note that in the years leading up to the opening of Crystal Beach Park in 1890, John E. Rebstock was involved in more meetings with Buffalo real estate developers and capital investors than he was with any officials from the Methodist Church or any other clerical body. Formal meetings and agreements with church officials and government representatives about chartering a religious assembly (the Crystal Beach International Assembly) would not take place until 1895. The C.B.I.A. is discussed later in this chapter.

In 1887, the sand on Crystal Beach was probably even whiter than it appears today. Even after a century or more of bonfires, lake vegetation, zebra mussels, and human activity, the sun still glistens off of the smooth, wind-flattened sand, making it look like millions of tiny diamonds. Regardless of how the name Crystal Beach came about and ended up in John Rebstock's head, the beauty of the sand, the sun sparkling off the water, and the view of Abino Bay remains as breathtaking today as it was when he first laid eyes on it as a young man in the 1850s.

The following is a list of other places across North America named Crystal Beach and the year they adopted the name in chronological order: Crystal Beach, Ontario (1888); Crystal Beach Park, Ohio (1906); Crystal Beach, Florida (1912); Crystal Beach, New York, (1929); Crystal Beach Park, Oklahoma (1936); Crystal Beach, Texas (1940); Crystal Beach near Nepean, Ontario (1960).

With all due respect to Charles O. Rano and all the other places named Crystal Beach, John E. Rebstock can be proud of the fact that he was the first person to successfully use the name, etching it into the memories of millions of people.

Source: Buffalo Enquirer, Aug. 1894

The simplified history that a "religious camp" or "colony" was the first thing that popped up in Crystal Beach in 1888 is historically inaccurate. While John E.'s *intention* was to eventually establish a Chautauqua-style religious camp, it never quite materialized until 1895, and even then, it only lasted two short seasons.

CRYSTAL BEACH: OUT OF THE PARK

The first visitors to the wooded grove and beach area were indeed campers, but not in the Chautauqua religious camp sense. They were literally camping in the woods, while enjoying the resort's attractions: Swings, slides, games, the merry-go-round, and concerts. Many of them could have very well also been doing so for spiritual purposes, and tent sermons and lectures were indeed held, but there was no formalized religious "assembly" or "camp" at that time.

John E. Rebstock was a deeply religious Methodist who had been a Sunday School superintendent with the Riverside Methodist Church in Buffalo. He had also seen the Wesleyan Methodist camp meetings in Martha's Vineyard. In addition, a Wesleyan Methodist Church was known to have existed in Bertie Township as far back as the early 1800s.

It is certainly likely that John Rebstock encouraged spiritual sermons and Sunday Schools within the grove. After all, his middle name was Evangelist. However, he simply could not ignore the drawing power of the amusements which simultaneously and spontaneously started forming a primitive midway north of the Oak Ridge bluff on the east side of the property.

In 1887, there was still no actual "Crystal Beach Amusement Park" in name yet. One of the earliest media accounts of John Rebstock's resort in "Point Abino" appears in August of 1890, when he was interviewed by a *Buffalo Courier* reporter on board the *Dove* as it sailed to Point Abino from Buffalo. Again, at that time the general lakeshore area of Bertie Township was generally referred to as Point Abino.

While the idea of a religious assembly may very well have been Rebstock's original goal when he acquired the property in 1887, as early as 1890 he was already promoting the area in the media as an amusement park-style resort. He referred to the resort as "picnic grounds" at the time.

Asked about his plans to upgrade his resort in Point Abino, he revealed that he was looking to purchase bigger and better steamboats to ferry passengers from Buffalo to "Crescent Beach" in Point Abino. The Courier article mentions that Rebstock had some time ago purchased "a fine tract of land at Point Abino" and that he intended to make "Coney Island out of Point Abino." Following the success of

Coney Island in New York, there had been a boom in the building of amusement parks across North America.

The article's multiple references to "Point Abino" rather than "Crystal Beach" is a clear indication that the place had not yet been officially named. This is supported within the same news article by the reporter repeatedly referring to the resort as "Crescent Beach at Point Abino." (Not to be confused with today's Crescent Beach at the end of Crescent Road in Fort Erie). Even the title of the article is "At Crescent Beach." The name Crystal Beach is not mentioned once in the entire piece. Perhaps the word "Crescent" would simply morph into the word "Crystal" after advice and input (and the ouster of Charles Rano) from Rebstock's influential Buffalo business partners.[4] Or, perhaps the reporter was simply hopelessly uninformed.

Looking back through the historical perspective of today, it is easy to simply assume that the area was called Crystal Beach from day one, but the name seems to have been settled upon sometime in 1890, after Rebstock's Buffalo investors came on board.

A handwritten letter from John E. Rebstock's daughter-in-law, Helen Rebstock, cites July 16, 1890 as the date of the maiden voyage of the *Dove*, and the opening day of Crystal Beach Amusement Park.[5] The *Dove* had in fact attempted to land at Crystal Beach a few days earlier during a test run, but could not successfully dock at the primitive pier. There is also evidence, including photographs, that the *Dove* had made several test-runs to the Point Abino and Crystal Beach area as early as 1889.

In its first year, Crystal Beach was nothing more than a sandy shoreline with a crude wooden dock, and two water toboggan slides at the beach. The sand bluff on the west side of where the cut through the dune would be made was called Maple Ridge. This would come to be called the 'Hill' in later years, dotted with summer homes along the beachfront for generations of Western New Yorkers. The dune to the east was called Oak Ridge, north of which would be the original midway. At one time, there would be over thirty cottages along the top of this ridge. Most of these cottages were demolished in 1924 when the Oak Ridge was partially levelled by fire hoses and the sand used to back-fill behind the new giant sea wall.

Once through the cut, the grove extended around the north side of the bluff to both the east and the west. To the west, campers would cross a rustic bridge over a small ravine, and follow a natural footpath through the shaded sandy tract. Guests would emerge from the wooded area on the north side of the dune into Maple Grove, where today there exists a parking lot and Erie Road, both of which were non-existent at the time. This is where the picnic area, the assembly grounds, and the amphitheatre were located.

Here, visitors would relax in white canvas tents or attend lectures, sermons, and musical recitals in the pavilions. Rough wooden bleachers were eventually installed on the north face of the dune, creating a natural outdoor amphitheatre. This was located somewhere within the Maple Grove, between the cut and where the new Hotel Royal would be built in Bay Beach in June of 1900. A crude, hand-drawn map from 1894 shows an open-sided octagonal pavilion-like structure, along with two other open-air structures in this location.

To the east, the grove extended towards Ridge (now Ridgeway) Road, however, east of the cut would eventually become part of the main midway. Rebstock appears to have wanted a separation between the spiritual pursuits and the entertainment activities. There were picnic pavilions and swings in this area also. Kiddie Land, and the future picnic grove, would eventually be located in the north part of this area. The same 1894 map depicts a baseball diamond and athletic field in the far eastern end of the grove, just on the west side of Ridge Road.

On very early maps of the resort, the pathway known as "the cut" extended directly north from the lake in the same longitudinal line that Derby Road would one day follow. It transitioned into a primitive dirt road that went right up the middle of Lot 25, Broken Front Concession, which was the Rebstock property. Further north, as one emerged from the grove, is described as the "fine farm of John Rebstock, the President of the Crystal Beach Steamboat Company."[6] The dirt road continued north into the open fields of the Rebstock farm, eventually cresting the ridge at Rebstock Road, where John E.'s residence was located.

A quick left turn of his horse and carriage, and he was home. Rebstock had to get to work somehow, and his most likely commuting route was along this pathway from his residence directly into the heart of the early resort. John E., as park superintendent (in addition to being ticket-taker and boat pilot), had an office at Emerson's Supply House well within the park grounds. Rebstock's well-worn pathway was the early beginning of Derby Road, the name of which would actually come later. In the early days of the resort, it was known as Central Road.

The first store in Crystal Beach, Harry B. Emerson's Supply House, was located on the southernmost section of this early version of Derby, as early as 1890. It was within the future park grounds, where the miniature railway station would come to be. This store evolved into the Family Supply store (the second version of the "Supply House"). The Emersons ran the store during the summer months for the campground visitors, then would re-locate to Ridgeway for the winter. The Park Superintendent, the Magistrate, as well as a barber shop, a laundry, and Crystal Beach's first post office (all run by Edward Buck), had offices in or near the Supply House at one time. Through the years, Ed Buck also served Crystal Beach as a Village Trustee, Justice of the Peace, and Postmaster.

CRYSTAL BEACH: OUT OF THE PARK

The Supply House, circa 1900.

L to R: Sarah Scott, unknown, John Young (Customs Officer), May Emerson, Rebstock children? unknown, Harry Emerson, Mr. Reavley, J.E. Rebstock, unknown.

Photo: Courtesy Cathy Herbert

Haun's Mill, built in 1876 by Charles Herbert Haun, supplied most of the lumber to build and expand both the park and the village. It was west of and adjacent to the Rebstock farm, and at that time, west of Elmwood on Rebstock. The route down the future Derby Road was also undoubtedly the same one taken by Mr. Haun's fleet of wagons when delivering the hundreds of loads of lumber needed to keep up with the expansion of the resort. The business partnership between the Haun Mill and the amusement park lasted for over one hundred years. Of course, once John Rebstock designed the formal layout of the village, Derby Road's southern terminus was established at the newly-created Erie Road.

By 1891, things started picking up at Crystal Beach. The steamer *Pearl* was doing six trips a day, and the Crystal Beach Hotel (later named the Belleview, then the Bon Air) was built high up on the bluff above the dock.

A bathing house, a carousel, and—eventually—a small scenic roller coaster were added, along with more pavilions. Behind the dune in the grove, an amphitheatre with a crude tent-like roof was erected somewhere near the future corner of Derby and Erie Roads.

Visitors, or "campers" as they were referred to, pitched canvas tents on wooden platforms, much like the ones seen in old Civil War photographs. People literally camped in the grove for extended stays of relaxation and sun-bathing, like they still do in summer cottages in Crystal Beach over a century later. These folks were the very first incarnations of the Crystal Beach summer resident. Some came for the sermons, some for the fun, but many simply enjoyed camping in the woods for relaxation and spiritual rejuvenation.

After the village and the park became supplied with abundant natural gas lines, and the dynamo at the Haun mill became operational, camping in the woods at Crystal Beach did not always involve the traditional outdoor hardships. Wood camp fires were possible, but many of the campsites were also equipped with gas jets and had access to electricity. It could be referred to as one of the earliest versions of "glamping."

In the air there would have been sounds of hymns being sung, sermons, and lectures. However, the cry of the barkers, the music of the carousel's orchestrion, and the squeals from the water toboggans would have surely enticed campers over to the midway and the beach where all the fun was taking place.

In the days before building codes, zoning bylaws, and planning departments, the wooden tent platforms would eventually form the floors of more permanent but crude wooden "cottages." Some would rent or purchase lots from John Rebstock and build the very first versions of Crystal Beach cottages. Some of these early cottages are still standing in the village today.

CRYSTAL BEACH: OUT OF THE PARK

In the early days, there was no Erie Road, and the tents and cottages were scattered throughout the southern end of the Rebstock property and within the grove. Cottages also started being built "around the bend [of the shoreline] clear up to Point Abino Beach," before Erie Road even existed.[7] These folks would have been ferried from the boat landing by water taxi across the bay to their summer homes. In the early days there was the *Abino*, and later the *Marion L*, operated by Charles "Ike" Adams. Alternatively, they could opt to take Web Haun's horse-drawn taxi, nicknamed the *Black Mariah*, along the beach out to the Point.

By the early 1890s, John Rebstock had drawn up plans for a fully laid-out village, with the radial-spoke street pattern that still exists today. This plan was proposed as an *extension* of the existing summer resort, which at the time was simply called Crystal Beach. The name for the proposed extension to the north was Crystal Park, confirming that the resort pre-dated the actual village in using the name Crystal Beach, and that the circular road design of the village came well after the establishment of the park and grove areas closer to the lake.

Lots were divided off, Erie Road was created, physically separating the village area from the resort area. Cottages and buildings started going up along the narrow, primitive roads almost immediately. Religious sermons were still conducted in the grove area at that time, with services at the amphitheatre, or in some of the many platformed canvas tents set up by the campers.

It has been speculated that Rebstock may have envisioned the Queens Circle becoming the centre for worship services, but contrary to popular belief, the Circle never took on that role. In fact, an early 1890s village plan map shows the Circle with plans for a dining hall and kitchen in the centre, not a church or tabernacle.

Although quite primitive compared to its coming glory years, Crystal Beach was already well into its operation as an amusement park when in 1895, John Rebstock and others announced the formation of the Crystal Beach International Assembly. Media reports state that the formation of this assembly had been under consideration for some time.[8] This was the first formal and organized attempt at establishing a

Chautauqua-style assembly at Crystal Beach. The group's mission was stated as being "dedicated to the educational and religious development of its patrons."

The assembly was modeled after other well-known religious camp assemblies such as Cottage City, Chautauqua, Silver Lake, and Grimsby, Ontario. The two-month non-denominational educational and religious program was to take place in the grove, entirely apart from the Crystal Beach Steamboat Company grounds and its distractions:

> The organisation will stake out large grounds in the woods at Crystal Beach, entirely apart from the property owned by the Crystal Beach Steamboat Company, and about a five or ten-minute walk from the boat landing, and will build a large platform with stationary seats, and put up a large tent that will seat 2,500 to 3,000 people. The Assembly will be opened July 1, Dominion Day.[9]

Reverend W.H. Main of Emmanuel Baptist Church was selected as President, and Dr. R.T. Snyder (Ph.D., Doctor of Divinity) of Preston, Ontario, was chosen as Chancellor. Several recognizable local names served as the first board of managers, including John E. Rebstock, C. H. Haun, Eber Cutler, and W. B. Dixon. The opening of the first session of the Assembly on Dominion Day 1895, was attended by many dignitaries, including W. H. Montague, M.P., who was also Canada's Secretary of State at the time. More than forty speakers were scheduled for the first summer session, and some of the educational offerings included a school of stenography, and German language classes.[10]

The building of a new hotel was announced. It would be called the Assembly House and would serve as the C.B.I.A.'s headquarters. Its exact location is lost to history. Indicators are that it was facing present-day Erie and Derby Roads, probably within the park grounds, where other buildings had also been located prior to Erie Road being built.

Nearby, the assembly's outdoor 3000-seat tent-covered amphitheatre would be used for larger sermons, lectures, and entertainment.

Access to it would be from the south, directly from the cut, as visitors came off of the walkway, and also from the rustic bridge.

Interestingly, Chancellor Snyder, the religious man, was also a shrewd businessman. He became the owner of the Assembly House, then later the Hotel Royal, and would eventually come to own an entire block of buildings on Erie Road that would be known as the Snyder Block.

The 1895 photo below is a view from just inside the south edge of the Queens Circle, looking south down Derby Road at the "Rustic" on the right, one of the first cottages in Crystal Beach. On the left side of the road are some of the first houses in Crystal Beach. Beyond the Rustic to the right within the trees, was the grove. Straight down Derby was the cut, where the giant dune separated the grove from the beach.

Photo: Courtesy Cheryl Fretz Carlyle

The two boys in the buggy are John E.'s sons Arthur, 14, and Walter, 12. The boy on the road further to the right is 10-year-old George J. Rebstock. It is unknown who the man in the other buggy is. It could very well be John E. himself. On the extreme left is a large canvas tent just outside of the circle, possibly a sermon tent, but by no means one with a capacity of three thousand people.

As there was no official political structure in Crystal Beach yet, and the property belonged to John Rebstock, the large ornate buildings in the middle-left background may have been affiliated with the Crystal Beach International Assembly, which Rebstock helped start.

It appears to be close to the location where the future Municipal Hall would be at Belfast and Lincoln. An early 1890s map, however, shows tennis courts being planned for that location. It does not appear to be a residence, unless it is one of the hybrid tent-cottages which were popular in Crystal Beach at the time, both in the grove and around the Rebstock property.

The centre portion of the building appears to be some sort of pavilion or tent-like structure, with arched open side windows. The roof area of the larger building appears to have large vent-flaps on it. In his 1978 booklet, George J. Rebstock (John E.'s son) describes the Assembly House as being located at Derby and Ridge Roads, which is impossible as they both run north-south, parallel to each other.[11] Perhaps George J. meant "between" Derby and Ridge Roads, which is the approximate location of the structure in the photo. He also could have meant "near" Derby and *Erie* Roads, using the modern-day geographic reference for describing the location.

Adding to the historical confusion is the freely-used word "assembly" in reference to several entities in Crystal Beach. There was the "Crystal Beach International Assembly", the educational organization started in 1895. There was the "assembly grounds" which were located somewhere in the Maple Grove. Then there was the "Assembly House", an actual building somewhere near Derby and Erie, owned and run by Dr. Snyder, where the C.B.I.A. held its short-lived administrative meetings. In addition to all of this, the actual congregations of worshipers were also casually referred to as the "assemblies," which is exactly what they were: Catholic, Methodist, Protestant, and more.

After the idea of a religious and educational Chautauqua started losing steam, the Assembly House (C.B.I.A. headquarters) became the Assembly House Hotel. It remained quite popular long after the C.B.I.A. had ceased to operate in 1896, being mentioned in the Buffalo society columns as a frequent destination for many. It continued to host musical and dramatic performances, along with art exhibits, well after the C.B.I.A. had folded.

The Crystal Beach International Assembly, which had started with such optimism and fanfare in 1895, lasted no more than two summers.

There is no mention of it in the historical records or media reports after 1896.

It appears that the name "Assembly House" became a nomadic designation. An article written in 1952 by Peter Andrews of the *Buffalo Courier Express* describing the Assembly House is obviously referring to its later location at Bay Beach, which became the Hotel Royal:

> The Assembly House was on the beach front where the bathhouse is now, it was the largest of the hotels and was used for housing the entertainers. Later named the Royal, it was destroyed by fire in 1923.[12]

An article from 1899 announced that a Philadelphia syndicate, along with Dr. Snyder "who runs the Assembly House," will build a large elaborate hotel "on the shore, 1,000 feet to the west of the boat landing." This would be on the west side of the Schooley Road allowance, where the current Bay Beach complex is today.

The architect of the huge colonial-style building would be a 23-year-old from Buffalo, George W. Graves. He would gain fame for designing and building many prominent and historic buildings in the Detroit and Grosse Pointe areas of Michigan. The initial name announced for this new hotel on the beach was to be the Grand Royal Hotel. It may have initially been referred to as the Assembly House Hotel, in deference to its predecessor near Derby and Erie. Eventually, the name Hotel Royal was adopted. At the time that it was destroyed by fire, it was definitely named the Hotel Royal.[13]

Dr. Snyder would continue to run and host the "assemblies" at this new location, while his son Harry would open a steam laundry business at the same complex. Old village maps and early aerial photographs confirm the location of the Hotel Royal, along with the Royal Casino right at Bay Beach, immediately west of the Schooley Road allowance. The Hotel Royal also housed entertainers engaged at Crystal Beach.

The Hotel Royal, Bay Beach, circa 1908.

Photo: Fort Erie Public Library

Remnants of the foundation of the Royal Casino still exist today, underneath the new Bay Beach complex built by the Town of Fort Erie. While being rented out as summer apartments by the Rebstock family as recently as the 1990s, it was still referred to as the "Casino Building."

Throughout the early days of Crystal Beach, religious services were nomadic, having to be held at different venues—at first in tents in the assembly grounds, at the outdoor amphitheatre, at the Assembly House, at the roller rink above the midway, and even at private residences. While religion and amusement were the original plans for Crystal Beach, only one of them caught on with the campers and the general public.

In 1905, religious services in Crystal Beach became centralized at the newly-built St. George's Church on Ridgeway Road, well away from the midway. The People's United Church was also established on Derby Road. For decades after, summer residents and visitors joined the local population in worship on Sundays at both locations. John Rebstock now had the opportunity to focus solely on developing the entertainment side of the resort, in addition to his many other business interests.

In 1896, another new attraction called the Roof Garden was built, described as being well within the grove and diagonally across from the Assembly House. This description places it somewhere near the vicinity of Erie and Derby Roads.

The Roof Garden was the top floor of a beautiful two-storey building, entirely open with the exception of a floral-covered roof. Art exhibits and musical and dramatic performances took place there. Determining the exact location of this mysterious structure is beyond the scope of this book. Five bowling alleys, an athletic field, and a new dancing hall were also announced at this time.[14]

Whether Crystal Beach was originally a religious camp, a fledgling amusement park, or a co-existence of both, legally and politically it was still nothing more than a gathering place on a private farm located in Bertie Township.

While the religious and educational curriculum of the Crystal Beach International Assembly was planned by the organization, John Rebstock, as the property owner, designed the physical layout of the village itself. He based his design on the Wesleyan Methodist's religious camp meeting grounds in Cottage City on Martha's Vineyard. The concept was based on a central hub, with concentric ring roads surrounding it, and radial spokes extending out from it. Pitman Grove in New Jersey is another example of a religious camp meeting area with the radial spoke pattern layout.

Most of the historic Wesleyan Methodist camp meeting areas throughout the northeastern United States followed this same basic pattern. They were all part of the religious camp meeting movement of the early 19th century.

Cottage City is known today as Oak Bluffs, on Martha's Vineyard. It was laid out with a central pavilion or tabernacle, where the religious and educational services would take place, with pathways spreading out in a radial web-like pattern to other tented areas. It would be remiss not to discuss the curious similarities between Cottage City and Crystal Beach.

As a devout Methodist, it is likely that John Rebstock had observed the camp meeting areas in Martha's Vineyard during one of his many business trips to Massachusetts. John E. did in fact travel to the Boston area, and it is confirmed that in February 1886 he was in Boston to continue negotiations and to finalize a distribution contract with the Magee Stove Company. At the time, John E. owned the Rebstock Stove Company at 564 and 566 Washington Street in Buffalo.[15]

As the deal was described as having been in negotiations "for some time," he had likely made several trips to the Boston area prior to the finalization meeting in February of 1886. This particular trip to Massachusetts was made the year just prior to Rebstock acquiring the Bertie Township farm that would become his lakefront resort. Crystal Beach adapted a very similar look to that of Cottage City, although Rebstock refined it to a more orderly and symmetrical design.

At Cottage City, the central circular road where the sermons took place had other areas of tents surrounding it. One of these areas was the eerily-named Crystal Park, the same name John E. proposed for the Crystal Beach Park expansion, both in his early draft plans, and on proposal maps. Trinity Park Circle in Oak Bluffs is the core area of the original gatherings there, and today it still has a central pavilion within it. The Queens Circle in Crystal Beach follows the same inspiration and design. A Google Maps street-view tour of present-day Oak Bluffs will appear very familiar to anyone who knows the inner village streets of Crystal Beach.

> [Cottage City] developed in a radial-concentric pattern which was little used in America at that time. Paths radiating from Trinity Circle led to smaller circles where large groups of tents had been located.[16]

Ironically, Cottage City experienced the same phenomenon that Crystal Beach would experience. Visitors took more interest in the amusements and concessions springing up around the retreat than they did in the religious activities within the circle and surrounding area. Although they installed a carousel at Cottage City in 1884 which still operates today, the area did not evolve into a full-blown amusement park like Crystal Beach did.

The street layout of Crystal Beach is especially unique. Loomis, Conway, Lincoln, and Cambridge sounds like the name of a Washington, D.C. law firm, but those are the names of the four concentric roads surrounding the Queens Circle like rings in a puddle. Loomis Crescent once formed nearly a full circle inside of Lincoln, but ended at Shannon on the west side of Derby, and at Belfast on the east side.

Prior to being named Loomis sometime after the 1920s—likely after a member of the Loomis family, one of whom, Orland, lived on the street—it was named Crescent Road West and Crescent Road East on the northern half of the Circle, and Providence Lane (west side) and Windsor Lane (east side) on the southern half. Including the two pedestrian walk-throughs (Ulster Lane and Munster Lane), there are eight "spokes" radiating from the Queens Circle that extend out like spider legs, each in perfectly sectioned directions: North, North East, East, South East, and so on, like the points on a compass (see map below).

The village originally deemed the Circle as public reserve 'A' and today it is designated a community park. Four other public reserves were located at each rounded corner of Cambridge Road and still exist today. Three are deemed public open spaces. The northwest reserve 'B' is currently an active public park, once called Hébert Park by locals, but now named after former Fort Erie Mayor Madeline Faiazza. The northeast 'C' and southwest 'D' reserves are still open areas today and are considered passive public parks. The Crystal Beach Village Hall and Fire Hall were built on the southeast 'E' reserve, which is now privately owned.

Given John Rebstock's devout Methodist background, and that his original intention was to found a religious camp meeting, it is intriguing that the pattern he chose for the street layout in Crystal Beach also resembles the Ichthys Wheel or Christian Wheel Cross, which has been used historically in many other religions such as Hinduism and Buddhism, dating back to the second century. In Christianity, the Ichthys Wheel represents a Christian-centred life, with the strength and driving force of the wheel and spokes coming from the centre, or hub. This is where the religious services took place in the Wesleyan camp meetings in the U.S. However, in Crystal Beach religious activities never left the grove area.

Rebstock originally laid out the streets, which were actually nothing more than narrow primitive footpaths, in this exact pattern, with the hope of drawing people towards the centre. His goal was to "popularize Christianity for the common people."[17]

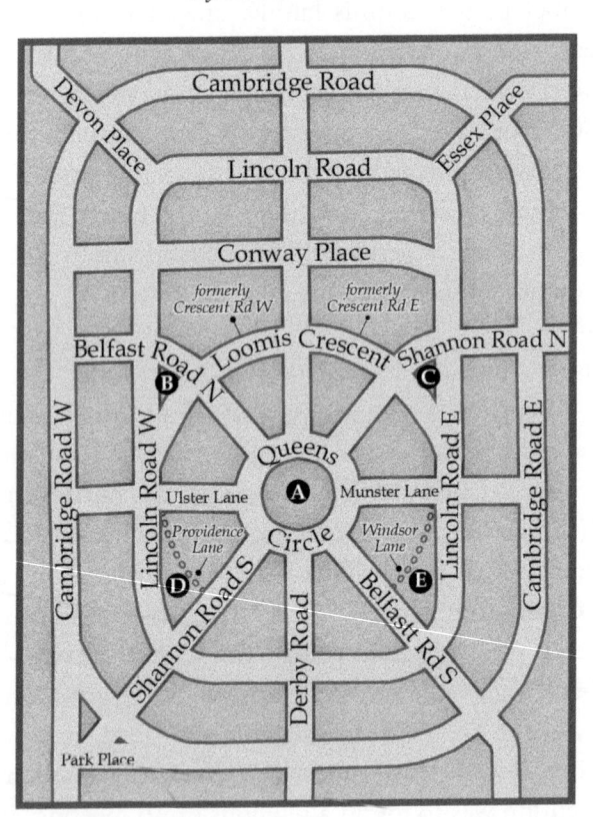

Crystal Beach core area.

Source: John Docker

Although he was obviously inspired by the pattern, it is unlikely that John E. Rebstock was aware of the historical religious significance of the Christian Wheel Cross design at that time. It is intriguing to wonder if perhaps even the founders of the Wesleyan Methodist camp movement itself were aware of the symbol's historic and religious significance. Perhaps it is simply innate human behaviour within communal settings to gravitate around a central core area, much like the fire pit in prehistoric times.

If true, the idea that the Village of Crystal Beach's physical layout was inspired by or based upon historic Christian principles, could be one of the greatest ironies in the history of the village, given some of the distinctly unholy events which would take place in the village over the ensuing decades.

Ironically, the eight-spoked wheel design is also a symbol which can represent chaos. At various times through the years this could also have been a very appropriate symbol for the village. Unfortunately, the "chaos" interpretation of the symbol arrived fairly recently from Michael Moorcock in the 1970s, some ninety years after John Rebstock's plan.

The affiliation between religion and circles in the early days of Crystal Beach is also referred to in George J. Rebstock's memoir, where he wrote that in 1905 the King's Daughters Circle was formed in Crystal Beach.[18] Although very tempting to skew or interpret this literally as being connected to the actual Crystal Beach village circle, it is more than likely that he was referencing a local chapter or "Circle" of the International Order of the King's Daughters group. His father had designed the actual circle years before. He does not mention where they held their meetings. Perhaps in the Queens Circle?

According to early village maps, the circle was called Queen Circle as early as 1893. The 's' was added at some later date, but without an apostrophe for some reason. It is also shown as Queens Place on C.J. Pilkey's 1921 map of the village, as well as other maps.

The Order of the King's Daughters was established in New York in 1886 by a group of Methodist, Episcopal, and Presbyterian women, and was an inter-denominational Christian organization dedicated to philanthropy. Their stated objective was "The development of Spiritual Life and Stimulation of Christianity." Very similar to John Rebstock's original objective for Crystal Beach.

Formed in New York City, the current international head of this organization is in Chautauqua, New York. State and provincial "Branches" are further divided into local unions or "Circles" of friendship, who meet monthly.[19] The group's symbol is the Maltese Cross which, like the Christian Wheel Cross, and the Queens Circle, is an eight-point cross.

Crystal Beach's Queens Circle is still a place to gather for many people, and it is a place of peace and tranquility. The Friends of Crystal Beach hold an annual event there appropriately called the Circle of Art, and there is a farmer's market on weekends. The atmosphere is very inviting and relaxing, and one has to wonder whether the people who stood there a hundred years ago had the same feeling of convergence that one feels today.

Crystal Beach B.I.A. Queens Circle Dedication Stone.

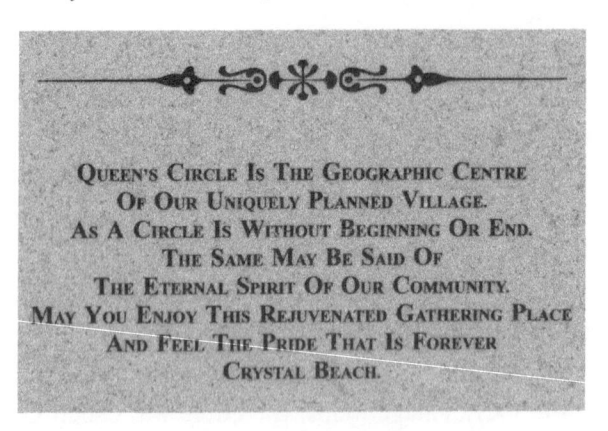

> QUEEN'S CIRCLE IS THE GEOGRAPHIC CENTRE
> OF OUR UNIQUELY PLANNED VILLAGE.
> AS A CIRCLE IS WITHOUT BEGINNING OR END.
> THE SAME MAY BE SAID OF
> THE ETERNAL SPIRIT OF OUR COMMUNITY.
> MAY YOU ENJOY THIS REJUVENATED GATHERING PLACE
> AND FEEL THE PRIDE THAT IS FOREVER
> CRYSTAL BEACH.

Written by Brad Murphy

In the early 1890s, Crystal Beach implemented another long-standing tradition from Cottage City called the Grand Illumination, which has been celebrated there since the 1860s, and still exists today. Initially rejected by the Wesleyan Methodist campers there, they eventually came to embrace the tradition.

The concept of a Grand Illumination is simply the simultaneous display of many sources of light to commemorate a special occasion. Christmas lights are one example of an annual community "Grand

Illumination." In Cottage City, the Grand Illumination began as part of the Cottage City Carnival, an annual August event since 1868. It involves a parade and thousands of illuminated Asian lanterns on people's cottages and throughout parks, along with bonfires and fireworks.[20]

In Crystal Beach, the idea for a Grand Illumination was likely conceived by John Rebstock, perhaps once again being inspired by his visits to Cottage City. In 1891, natural gas lines were laid into the amusement park and the grove in preparation for the event on Saturday, July 4. Supply lines had been installed earlier in Crystal Beach to fuel the many gas lamps around the village, and the new lines would be left in place permanently to provide light, heating, and camping fires within the park and grove.[21]

Natural gas was inexpensive in Bertie Township at the time, as a large natural gas pocket had been discovered in 1889 in the Sherkston area. It was so abundant, in fact, that in the 1890s, the Provincial Gas Company would also supply Buffalo with natural gas via pipes laid across the Niagara River. The Provincial Gas Company would build an office at the corner of Derby and Queens Circle, which now houses an antique and collectible store.

Again in 1893, another Grand Illumination event called for a series of bonfires to be lit by the residents along the shore of "Crystal Bay" from Point Abino to the pier. The fires were to be lit upon the eight-thirty p.m. signal of six whistle blasts from the arriving *Canadiana*. Rafts with flaming tar barrels were also set adrift into the bay, adding to the dramatic effect of the illumination. During this same period of time, Grand Illuminations were also held at the Chautauqua Assembly resort in New York State. Point Abino residents hoped to make this event an annual affair, but the lack of historical records about it indicate that it never caught on.[22]

After attempting to promote the spiritual and mental uplift of the people, John Rebstock the businessman witnessed the resort visitors spending more time at the midway enjoying the amusements, and saw the writing on the wall. He noticed that "even the ministers and Sunday School teachers seemed to be more interested in the side shows than they were in the services." As an entrepreneur, he decided to capitalize. He shifted his focus to the building of an amusement midway along the lakeshore, with the goal of turning it into "Buffalo's Coney Island," as the U.S. media liked to call it.

Crystal Beach Boardwalk, 1908.

Photo: Courtesy Clark Family

The above photo is of the Crystal Beach Boardwalk, facing east from above the pier, and is a fascinating illustration of the longtime American influence in the park and the village. The forty-six stars in the one U.S. flag would make this scene likely the summer of 1908, as Oklahoma had recently become the forty-sixth state in November of 1907.

Concessions, amusements, swings, and a wooden boardwalk were the initial instalments. A merry-go-round was the first ride, then a Ferris wheel and a primitive miniature scenic railway. Then came more rides, bigger and faster, followed by daredevil acts, acrobats, fortune tellers, and vaudeville shows. Steady growth of the amusement park took place in the early 1900s. By 1910, including the rides, there were one hundred different attractions, including a dance pavilion, roller skating rink, and bowling alleys.[23]

CRYSTAL BEACH: OUT OF THE PARK

Mr. Rebstock's winter vacations in Florida certainly appear to be very well-deserved. His son George J. describes his father's work day during the summers when he was running the amusement park:

> My Father would get up at 6 o'clock and I would take him to the park where he would get the workmen started getting the grounds in shape or making dock repairs. He would catch the first boat to Buffalo and go to the Dock Office Terminal and arrange for picnics and see that the boats were ready for the passengers for the day. On the 2:15 boat he would return to the Beach and look after the operation of the park until the last boat left at 11:30 at night.[24]

In the beginning some visitors arrived over land via horse and carriage, or by train to Ridgeway. They would then take Alfred Willson's horse-drawn bus ride from there to the resort. Later, the Skerrett family would operate the Red Line bus service between Crystal Beach, Ridgeway, Fort Erie, and Bridgeburg. The Peace Bridge was still years away. Prior to the *Dove*'s first run, most visitors from the U.S. either crossed the Niagara River at Black Rock, or hired smaller boats out of Buffalo. People had been crossing the lake to the Point Abino area for years.

Rebstock acquired lake boats to ferry people back and forth from Buffalo to Crystal Beach and built a larger, yet very crude dock. The first boat was the *Dove*, which could carry over five hundred passengers, and was later replaced by the Pearl. The boats would land at the rickety pier, which was anchored with log supports sunken into cribs filled with boulders. Passengers disembarked via long wooden planks dropped from the side of the ships onto the pier.

On August 30, 1890, John Rebstock hosted the boys from the Buffalo Orphan Asylum as his special guests aboard the *Dove* for a trip to Crystal Beach for the day. Although some became seasick out on the lake, most of the boys thoroughly enjoyed their day of fun and Mr. Rebstock's kind hospitality.[25]

Creepy, the Crystal Beach Clown, 1916.

Source: Fort Erie Public Library

THE GLORY DAYS

Prior to the 1908 season, John Rebstock, while maintaining ownership of the property, sold the physical assets of the Crystal Beach Park to the Lake Erie Excursion Company. The new owners replaced the *Dove* and the *Pearl* with the much larger sister ships, the *Americana*, which ran from 1908 to 1929, and then Crystal Beach's most famous boat, the *Canadiana*, which ran from 1910 to 1956.

In 1921, the final Crystal Beach pier was built for the two large steamers. Most of the 1921 pier's large concrete structure still exists today.

CRYSTAL BEACH: OUT OF THE PARK

The Canadiana leaving Buffalo on her maiden voyage, 1910.

Source: NY Heritage Press

The two sister ships would bring millions of people to the retreat. After her maiden voyage in 1910, the *Canadiana* ran round trips to Crystal Beach for forty-six seasons, sometimes making ten excursions a day throughout the summer with up to three thousand passengers aboard each trip. She would also do three-hour Sunday evening lake cruises complete with live orchestras and "refreshments." The *Canadiana* was a magnificent two-hundred-foot-long vessel with three decks, slot machines, alcoholic beverages, and beautiful hardwood trimmings throughout the interior. Passengers could look down at the massive engines from the deck above.

There was an orchestra stage on board, and some of the best big bands in the world played on the boat. Harold Austin of Fredonia, whose orchestra played both the *Canadiana* and the Crystal Ballroom, is sometimes confused with another slightly more famous Harold, also from the Buffalo area. Harold Arlen—who went on to write "Somewhere Over the Rainbow" and co-write "Old Black Magic"— and his various groups, the Southbound Shufflers and the Yankee Six, played on board the *Canadiana,* at the Royal Casino in Bay Beach, and were also the house band at Crystal Beach in 1924 and 1925.

The other Harold, last name Austin, in addition to performing at Crystal Beach and on the *Canadiana*, was also hired by the park to manage both the dance pavilion and the Crystal Ballroom. He played at the Crystal Ballroom up until 1956.

Police on both sides of the border mutually agreed to stay off the Crystal Beach boats, and to allow the company to police their own vessels while in "international waters." This is both legally and nautically impossible, as there are no "international waters" in Lake Erie, just an imaginary dotted line marking the border. It was basically a local and unofficial "look the other way" policy on the part of both the Canadian and American authorities. With drinking, slot machines, and whatever other vices happening on the boats, they simply did not want that extra responsibility and headache. They were the park's boats, and the park was tasked with policing them. Local politicians were more than happy to have private Crystal Beach Park police officers sworn in by a local magistrate. This mitigated a lot of problems, and use of resources for both the village police and the local OPP.

Passengers could cross the lake dancing on the beautiful dance floor on the upper deck to the sounds of a world-class orchestra, then dance the rest of the night away at the Crystal Ballroom to a different orchestra.

The fun did not just go one way, either. Many Canadians from the surrounding areas would take the *Canadiana* in the other direction and spend the day or evening in Buffalo for shopping or dinner and a show, returning to Crystal Beach on the last boat of the evening. The *Canadiana* deserves a complete chapter or book unto herself, and the existing literature about the vessel available online and in books is quite extensive and fascinating to read.

CRYSTAL BEACH: OUT OF THE PARK

Crystal Beach Amusement Park Arcade Token.

Made by my father for my mother as teenagers, 1947 (Author)

In 1924, Rebstock, having already sold the physical assets of the park in 1908, sold his remaining interest in the amusement park and the land to the Buffalo and Crystal Beach Company, of which George C. Hall was a member. Hall, a longtime concessionaire at the park, had started out by selling peanuts and popcorn from carts, then added suckers and candy kisses. He expanded his operations from those humble beginnings into owning many concessions and rides at Crystal Beach. Over one hundred years later, Hall's candy business is still in operation today under the ownership of local businessman Bob Steckley. The B. & C.B.C. began ambitious expansion and development plans for the park. The wooden board walk was replaced by a thousand-foot concrete seawall and promenade, much further out from the shoreline, then back-filled with sand. This created more usable land area for rides and attractions. The Crystal Ballroom, followed by Crystal Beach's two signature rides, the Cyclone in 1926, followed by the Comet in 1948, were subsequently built and thrilled generations of people over the next several decades.

After the extensive improvements, the park entered its glory years. By 1948, George Hall had acquired full ownership, and he and his family took the amusement park to the next level. The glory days lasted well into the 1950s and 1960s, and the Hall gentlemen of Point Abino became the Kings of Crystal Beach.

Rebstock went on to start the Bay Beach Park development west of Schooley Road, bringing hundreds more summer residents to the cottages and homes he and his sons and partners would build there. He was also the president of the Crystal Beach Board of Trade.

Another one of Mr. Rebstock's business ventures at this time was his thirty-acre apple, pear, and cherry orchard that he operated on his farm. It was known as one of the finest orchards in Welland County, supplying both local markets and large canneries with fruit. A de-humidifying/evaporating plant was built within the cavernous Rebstock barn, employing dozens from around the area.

In the middle of this orchard stood one of the oldest trees in the province of Ontario. The tree was a popular sight for tourists for many years. It was taken down in 1952 when Crystal Beach Public School was built. A similar huge, ancient tree that grew in the same school yard, stood for many years longer.

In addition to his stove company and real estate businesses, John Rebstock also ran a successful hardware business, was a partner in the Shepard-Rebstock Grocery Store, and even started a barrel-making company in 1903 in Waynesville, North Carolina.[26] Perhaps John E. had discovered Waynesville on one of his long, brutal road trips to his other resort project in Crystal Beach, Florida.

Presciently, fourteen years earlier in 1889, John E. had purchased twelve thousand acres of timberland in North Carolina and Virginia. Did he buy the forest in 1889, dreaming of one day opening a barrel company nearby? Unlikely, but if so, it was an incredible example of business foresight. Only John E. Rebstock knows for sure. News reports of the purchase stated that he planned to put the timber, which was mostly gumwood, into the market, and that he and his investors planned to start a new city some distance from Norfolk.[27] It is unknown if this planned city ever came to be, or what it may be named today.

In 1913, Rebstock was asked about his Crystal Beach, Florida development and how it was faring. Ever the promoter and entrepreneur, he replied, "Lots are being sold, fine homes have been erected, the weather is delightful, and the fishing was great. I caught so many fish, I am ashamed to look another one in the eye."[28]

In 1938, in keeping with the family's entrepreneurial spirit, John E.'s son, George J. started the Rebstock Insurance Company for something to do in the off-season. The business ended up serving the community at large for over eighty years.

The Comet, 1980s.

Photo: Dale Roddick

In the early days, the park had the most incredible array of circus-like daredevil acts, thrill rides, theatres, vaudeville shows, and full orchestras. Aerialists, skydivers, and side shows. A family of Japanese acrobats had their own theatre on the Midway. The park even boasted an actual human cannon ball. Victoria Zacchini of the acrobatic Zacchini Family would be fired from a cannon and land in a giant safety net during the 1946 and 1947 seasons. The park police chief, William Diamond, had the honour of assisting Miss Zacchini with her egress from the giant net.[29]

In a 1951 *Maclean's* magazine article by Thomas Walsh, owner Ed Hall describes seeing three thousand or more people get off of the *Canadiana* on a busy day. In the 1950 season, when over a million people visited the park, more than 250,000 people rode the Comet.

The *Maclean's* reporter was given the extremely modest figure of $250,000 by Hall as total park revenue for the year of 1951. Although quite substantial for that time, considering the millions of visitors and the numerous cash-only transactions at Crystal Beach Park, it is almost certain that Mr. Hall was either being very shy about the park's actual income, or he had the world's greatest accountant.

To those with knowledge of the inner workings of the amusement park's financial operations, the figure of $250,000 as total revenue is highly doubtful, and was likely several times that amount. After all, Maclean's was a nationally published magazine, and it was not a very good idea for an American businessman to publicly brag in a Canadian magazine about how much money he was making within Canada. That would just be asking for an audit.

In the 1950s, twenty-five thousand people in one day at the park was not uncommon. A lot of cash exchanged hands within the park, and the park owners would employ undercover Pinkertons Agency detectives to watch for thefts and any gaming or financial irregularities. This was a shrewd move by the park owners. As private contractors to the park, any financial irregularities that the Pinkertons detected would become strictly the park's information to do with, and act upon, as they pleased, as opposed to the consequences and negative publicity of involving the police, and likely the press. Similar to the policing arrangement on the Crystal Beach boats.

Since liability insurance was difficult to obtain for amusement parks in general, detailed signed incident reports would be meticulously filled out by any guests reporting even the smallest of injuries, or damage and loss of personal items. These were to have on hand in the event of the inevitable lawsuits.[30]

THE VILLAGE

After its beginnings as a piece of barren farmland in Bertie Township, where people would gather in the summer for recreational or spiritual purposes, the area known as Crystal Beach was designated a Police Village on December 7, 1898, pursuant to the Municipal Act of Ontario. Police Village was a term used in Ontario at the time to designate communities without a police force having at least 150 residents, but not more than five hundred acres in area. This was Crystal Beach's first political designation. The first trustees administering the Crystal Beach Police Village were Edward Leslie, Patrick Ryan, Charles Butler, and Edward Buck, who would also become the first postmaster.

Once the amusement park started doing well financially, the trustees and a group of citizens, John Rebstock included, started organizing efforts to have Crystal Beach incorporated into a town or village. At the time, John E. Rebstock was the President of the Crystal Beach Board of Trade. There had been previous petitions to the County to incorporate as a town by the Crystal Beach community, but they were unsuccessful in convincing the decision makers in Welland County.

At that time, to qualify as a town a petitioning community had to have at least two thousand people within a 500-acre boundary, while a village designation required 750 people within the same size area. The Crystal Beach petitioners claimed it was unfair that the census in Crystal Beach was always conducted in January or February, when there would be barely fifteen souls enumerated. Even John E. Rebstock left in the winter. He was indeed in Crystal Beach in February, but it was at his Crystal Beach, Florida resort. No one lived in Crystal Beach in the winter.

The group argued that if the Crystal Beach census was taken in July or August it would easily register fifteen thousand people or more, qualifying them as either a town or a village. There was, of course, vehement resistance to this from Bertie Township, as they would stand to lose all of the tax revenue which the park had been paying to them since being opened.

The Midway in Winter, looking west, 1911.

Photo: Courtesy Clark Family

If incorporated, the Village of Crystal Beach would become the sole recipient of the municipal taxes paid by the amusement park, as the park fell within the proposed village boundaries. It was argued that this increased revenue was both needed and deserved by Crystal Beach due to the costs of roads, sidewalks, and policing as a result of the increased summer population.

Prior to incorporation these additional costs had been born by the property owners in the Police Village area. The trustees directed Charles Shepard, C. J. Pilkey, and John Page, all members of the movement towards villagehood, to immediately begin the Crystal Beach census in August of 1919. Obviously, thousands of Americans would still be present in the village and would thus be enumerated.

The original 340-acre area petitioned for inclusion within the proposed village boundary consisted of all 180 acres of the Rebstock farm, which is the core area of present-day Crystal Beach. It also included ninety acres of the Haun farm, twenty acres of the Schooley farm, and fifty acres of the Brackbill and Claus farms. Of the 340 acres within the proposed village boundary, the amusement park would occupy thirty-seven acres. John E. Rebstock predicted a building boom in Crystal

Beach in 1921, and he turned out to be correct.[31] Real estate sales went off the charts.

After coming up with their creative solution regarding the census issue, the Village of Crystal Beach was incorporated in 1921. Charles Fletcher Swayze, Niagara MPP (Labour Party) sponsored the bill to obtain provincial approval of the designation. George Mathewson was named as the very first Reeve (similar to Mayor) of Crystal Beach. The first village council members were Councillors Charles Shepard, Emile Cuslin, J.H. Nagel, and George J. Rebstock. Also appointed were Clerk-Treasurer Frank Millington, Assessor H.B. Corey, Medical Health Officer Dr. George Stewart, Board of Health Member Walter J. Rebstock, Chief of Police William Scott, and Patrolmen Jacob Lown and William Barnhart.

A village was born. In 1921, tax and permit revenue allowed the village to install three miles of new sidewalks, streetlights, a sewage system, water works, and provide garbage collection and street cleaning services.[32] The village and the amusement park began a long-term mutually beneficial partnership.

The official Crystal Beach logo (creator unknown) includes all aspects of the village. There is a 'crystal' ball containing sunbathers, a ferry boat, a Ferris wheel, and a fun house all surrounded by maple leaf laurels, topped by the King's crown.

In the late 1800s, Crystal Beach's first roads were obviously not designed with the automobile in mind. They were intended for horse-and-buggy and foot traffic around the area, and to the bathing beach and amusements. They began simply as worn-down sandy foot paths. To this day the village streets remain quite narrow with the houses very close together. The close-in physical characteristics of the inner village roads help explain the tight-knit fabric that the core community has enjoyed over the decades.

Crystal Beach Village crest.

Source: From village letterhead

Parents throughout the village were the eyes, ears, and information network for each other in regards to the kids in the village. If you were causing trouble, you could be sure that your parents would know all about it before you even got home. In addition to everyone knowing everyone else's business, inside the Cambridge Road ring was also a tough place for a kid to grow up.

There were many summer cottages in the core area, then they started spreading further west and into Bay Beach. East of Ridgeway Road, residents were spared from the majority of the noise and parties, which usually took place over on one of the "Wood" streets, Cherrywood, Elmwood, Oakwood, Ashwood, Eastwood, etc.

The amusement park had its own volunteer firefighting brigade as early as 1911, consisting of park employees and concessionaires. Their water source was the 350,000-gallon reservoir located high up on the bluff behind the Hotel Bon Air. The police village followed suit in 1913, and started its first volunteer fire brigade with John E. Rebstock as president and his son Carl as secretary. This was initiated after Rebstock's house had burned to the ground in April of that year. A hat was passed at the initial meeting and $1,000 was collected to purchase fire fighting equipment.[33] Henry Oges, another one of the Beach's earliest and most industrious residents, was named fire chief and Edward Schuman and Malcolm McAlpin were named his assistant chiefs. Mr. Oges had started as a concessionaire selling soft drinks in the park, and like John Rebstock, became involved in many business ventures, including real estate rentals and sales.

After incorporation in 1921, the first official Crystal Beach Volunteer Fire Department was founded in 1925, with Charles Soper named as chief. It still serves the community as Station 6 of the Fort Erie Fire Department. Starting in the 1950s the Kinsmen Club, many of whom were also firefighters, provided ambulance services to the village and surrounding area for over twenty years.

Most of the firefighters were also the social and political leaders within the community, and members of the local service clubs. The solidarity within the Crystal Beach Volunteer Fire Department is illustrated during a community crisis in 1951, as described in a later chapter.

CRYSTAL BEACH: OUT OF THE PARK

Crystal Beach Volunteer Fire Department, 1960s.

Front: E. Heximer, A. Opatovsky, T. Pepper Sr., C. Martin, T. Everett, B. Gibbs, F. Blackley, A. Thornton, K. Thomson, F. Ward, A. Taylor, Back: u/k, J. Kosakowski, T. Pepper Jr., L. Szilagyi, B. Matthews.

Photo: Courtesy Frank Thornton

This same group of men coached hockey and baseball, held community fundraisers, carnivals, and street dances. Along with their spouses, they formed the backbone of the community. It was worse to get caught troublemaking by one of these gentlemen than it was to get caught by the local police. For almost one hundred years, the volunteers of the C.B.V.F.D. have risked their lives to keep the village safe, and have contributed thousands of hours towards advancing the community.

One young Crystal Beach man, who served both his community and his country, made the ultimate sacrifice in World War One. Robert James Burd, son of Henry and Sarah Burd of Crystal Beach, was killed in action at the Battle of Ypres in France on May 9, 1917. An engraved stone honouring his memory sits in the Queens Circle, and his name is also inscribed on the Canadian National Vimy Memorial in France. A play about his life, *Bobby Burd*, was written by Carrie Fox.

Another son of Crystal Beach, Warrant Officer John Richard Rebstock, the grandson of founder John E., was shot down and killed in North Africa during World War Two. A fighter pilot with the Royal Canadian Air Force, he is laid to rest in the Benghazi War Cemetery in Lybia, Africa. He was extremely popular and well-liked in his home village of Crystal Beach, but there are no memorials in his honour.

More recently, Corporal Albert Storm, while serving with the 1st Battalion, Royal Canadian Regiment of the Canadian Army, was killed in Afghanistan on November 27, 2006. He is honoured with a memorial playground at Waterfront Park.

At various times through the years, even in the winter, Crystal Beach supported two grocery stores, a hardware store, a planing mill, a movie theatre, a roller rink, a community centre with an outdoor hockey rink, and many, many drinking establishments. Both the park and the village had early-morning cleaning crews who kept the park and the streets clean for the summer. The village had gas street lamps as early as the 1890s, due to the cheap natural gas supply in the area.

Before the park built its own power generation house, an electric dynamo at the Haun Mill supplied both the park and the village with electricity. The village also had its own sewer system and water works. There was even a state-of-the-art fire alarm system throughout the village with four alarm boxes, each one strategically positioned in a different quadrant of the village. It was an autonomous, fully-functioning little village, with its own unique economy, gas and electricity supply, social life, and political structure. A futuristic model village, perhaps.

Many of the drinking establishments sponsored softball, darts, euchre, and other leagues, all which involved patronizing the sponsoring establishment. The large number of taverns, draft rooms and bootleggers throughout the decades in Crystal Beach combined with the high seasonal unemployment in the winter, led to alcoholism being a serious issue for many families in the village.[34]

CRYSTAL BEACH: OUT OF THE PARK

At one point, there was the Ontario Hotel, the Imperial Hotel, the Lincoln—which obtained one of Ontario's first liquor licences—the Park Hotel, the Derby, the Teal's, the Crystal Hotel, the Hébert's, and Sheehan's—which later became the Palmwood—just to name a few.

The Palmwood, which became a local landmark for drinking and dining, was a longtime lakeside dining and drinking establishment, with an outdoor patio overlooking the water. During the daytime and dinner hours, both the dining room and the outdoor patio would be packed with summer residents and locals out for happy hour or the Friday fish fry. In the summer it had a breezy, beachy atmosphere with plenty of Hawaiian shirts and flip-flops, and a stunning panoramic view of the lake and the Buffalo skyline. You could sip your beer and watch the Buffalo Canoe Club's sailboat races out on the water while you waited for your order.

In the late 60s, local legend Jack Gage opened a bar in the basement of the Palmwood. He and his buddies came up with the name "Circus by the Sea" and for over three decades it was indeed just that, a circus. On Friday and Saturday night it was the happening place to be for the young crowd from across the Niagara Region and Western New York. At times the lineup to get into the Circus on a Friday night would snake up the stairs, out of the parking lot, and down the street for two or three hundred metres. Along with the Palmwood upstairs, it was the centre of the action for the party crowd of all ages in Crystal Beach for decades.

One busy Friday night in the mid-80s, two armed robbers burst into the Circus, and put an immediate halt to the party by blowing the speakers of the sound system out with several blasts from sawed-off shot guns. They demanded the money from the tills, getting some, but not all of it. Thankfully, no one was hurt. The robbers took what they could and ran. They were later caught and convicted. Fun times on a Friday night at the Circus.

Crystal Beach's other infamous armed robbery occurred at the Imperial Bank of Commerce on Derby Road in the 1970s. Despite everyone in the village knowing who the perpetrators were, they were neither charged or prosecuted. No witnesses.

These watering holes gave way in later years to places like Sneakers (once the Teal's Hotel), the Paddy Wagon (once Vicky Loraine's Hair Salon), Southcoast (once Brodie's Drug Store and the Small Fry), the Crystal Chandelier, Oliver's, Exiles, and Lino's. That is an astonishing number of drinking places for only a one-square-mile area. Even with so many bars around the village, they all did well year-round, but especially in the summer. One of the biggest differences between the village and the park however, was that in the village alcohol was consumed voraciously, but in the park alcohol was strictly prohibited from day one.

Over the period of its one-hundred-year existence, there have been hundreds of millions of visitors from across the world who have been to either Crystal Beach Amusement Park or the beach. Dozens of books, filled with incredible photos, have been published about the park over the years. We all know that feeling of melancholy and nostalgia for a particular place and time in one's life, and Crystal Beach Amusement Park was that place and time for millions of people. Social media, books, and fan pages give thousands the chance to reminisce about their experiences there, back when they were young. There are Crystal Beach Amusement Park experts who know every detail about every ride. A million visitors per season was a common attendance figure during the park's heyday, and it operated for one hundred years. That's close to half a billion memories.

Crystal Beach Amusement Park and Stadium, 1949.

Photo: Courtesy Cathy Herbert

CRYSTAL BEACH: OUT OF THE PARK

In the early days, people arrived in Crystal Beach by horse and carriage, or by small boats from Buffalo, then via the larger steam ships from Buffalo, which was an experience unto itself. The steamships got bigger, and more people started arriving by car after the Peace Bridge was built in 1927. Even more arrived by fleets of busses bringing thousands of park-goers to the annual company picnics or community days from the Western New York area. Each and every one of them were touched in some way by the magical carnival on the beach.

The majority of visitors would probably describe Crystal Beach simply as an amusement park. That's the experience that they associate with the words "Crystal Beach." One thing is certain though. Crystal Beach looked very different from the outside than it did from the inside.

Although they numbered in the millions, very few amusement park visitors ever ventured outside the boundaries of the actual park grounds. Those who did leave the park area usually did so to rent a swimsuit and spend a few hours at the beautiful sandy beach. Visitors to the park rarely, if ever, ventured outside to wander around the village streets sightseeing. In the very early years this may have been a practice, but as the village matured into a community, tourists walking around sightseeing wasn't a common sight in the village. It also wasn't encouraged.

Of course, some would venture out of the main entrance of the park to experience the fast-food joints along Derby Road. Derby had once been the bustling business and commerce centre of the village. In later years, it evolved into "Hot Dog Alley", a unique strip of walk-up open-air fast-food joints on one side of the street and the Ontario Hotel, a popular watering hole, on the other side. There was also a great sit-down place in Hot Dog Alley, favoured by everyone who came to the Beach, known as Louie's Small Fry.

Derby Road 1920.

Derby Road 1970s.

Source: Fort Erie Public Library

Photo: Paul Kassay

It was always entertaining to grab a bite to eat at the Tropical Hut food stand at bar-closing time, right across from the Ontario Hotel. The great food came with an even better show, featuring the Crystal Beach OPP officers emptying the draft room of the Ontario of the usual guests who always refused to leave at closing time. In the summer in Crystal Beach, there was entertainment to be found everywhere. Amusing as they were though, the park, the beach, and the food-stand shows were only surface views of real life in the Beach.

Cronfelt's Loganberry (aka Tropical Hut) 1960s, Hot Dog Alley.

Photo: Paul Kassay

CRYSTAL BEACH: OUT OF THE PARK

The millions of people who have been to Crystal Beach would simply describe it as how they had personally experienced it: either a fun-filled amusement park, a beautiful sand beach, or a summer residence—perhaps all three. However, there was another Crystal Beach that the summer visitors and thrill seekers probably didn't even know existed: the village, and the people who lived their everyday lives there.

The year-round residents of the Beach could best describe the overall experience of Crystal Beach: growing up there, working in the park, surviving the deserted winters, and experiencing day-to-day village life outside of the park, and away from the beach. These folks were involved in, and witnessed, the inner workings of the village political machine. They were members of the service clubs, the school board, and the fire department. They raised families there, and to the residents of the village, it was much more than just a circus. It was home.

To most year-round residents, the amusement park became akin to what the waterfalls were to a resident of Niagara Falls: A soothing, familiar background decoration and sound that was just always there, like wallpaper. Some locals rarely went to the park unless they had a job there. Who wanted to hang out at their work place on their own time? For many locals, however, it was the go-to date night place, which didn't involve having to drive anywhere. A round of miniature golf, a couple of rides, some photos from the arcade, and a Hall's sucker never failed to impress. Everyone just thought the park would always be there.

The daily background sounds of the park from May to September became ingrained in the local population's subconscious. In the early days the orchestrions, sermons and lecturers, along with midway barkers, were the background sounds. To more recent generations, the backdrop of sound came to include the clicking of the chain on the track of the Comet reaching its apex just before the initial dive towards the lake below. Lying in bed at night with the windows open, you could visualize exactly where the Comet was in its one-minute wild ride around the tracks just by the volume of the screams and the clicking of the tracks. The whistle from the engine on the miniature railway could also be heard for miles around on a still day.

At one point, a nine-p.m. curfew siren sounded each night in the village, signalling to kids younger than sixteen that it was time to go home. The sound of the curfew siren sent chills down your spine, as it sounded just like a World War Two air raid siren from the movies. Most kids were not even aware of what the consequences were for disobeying the 'siren'. Even so, every kid in the village blindly obeyed the siren and ran home.

The horn blast from the park, signalling the eleven o'clock closing time, could also be heard throughout the village and into Ridgeway. Back in the *Canadiana* days, the huge vessel would sound its ship's horn upon arrival of the first run of the day, letting everyone in the village know that it was eleven a.m. All of these unique yet familiar sounds became part of the sonic background to generations of Crystal Beach residents over the years.

In the summer, midnight in the village was a strange time, sort of like the witching hour. After the parked closed for the day at eleven p.m. and all the noises had stopped, it briefly seemed like everything in the village was winding down for the night. But this was just the lull between the park closing and the bars closing, when things would come back to life again. Midnight in the village meant that night-time was just beginning. When the bars emptied out at one a.m., Hot Dog Alley would be flooded with hungry drunks. Afterwards, the private cottage parties would start up, bonfires would be lit along the beach, and drunken skinny-dippers would cool off in the lake.

Walking along Erie Road on a summer day, up Hot Dog Alley, or through the park, would expose one to seeing thousands of strangers with smiles on their faces, along with the alluring aromas of the sucker and waffle stands, and the fast-food joints. The smell of fresh donuts on Sunday morning at Pep's Bakery on Derby is just as strong an olfactory memory as the waffle stand in the park is. Along Erie Road, passing by Surella's and Santora's pizza places was just as heavenly. Crystal Beach was so busy that the two families would come just for the summer to operate their pizzerias in Crystal Beach.

Along the beach it was the same. Thousands of smiling people enjoying a sunny day at the beach, with the unmistakeable scents of baby oil, cigarette smoke, and Coppertone, mixed with the layered sounds of laughter, distant motorboats, and the different Buffalo radio stations.

The shore's east-west orientation gave beachgoers the full exposure of the sun from the left side in the morning, straight overhead at midday, and from the right into the late afternoon while still facing the beautiful view of the lake. You could even stay late, turn your beach chair towards the west, and watch the sun set gloriously behind Point Abino. It was a great beach for people who loved the sun. And likely a dermatologist's delight.

A very gradual slope of the lake floor, with no drop-offs and several sand bars made Crystal Beach a perfect spot for beachgoers, especially kids, to safely enjoy a day at the beach. It was THE beach to be at in all of Western New York and Southern Ontario. It has repeatedly been rated as one of the best beaches in North America in various polls of unknown source or reliability.

Even some of the rides in the park had their own unique smell, which added to their mystique, especially the Laff in the Dark. It had an oily, damp, burnt-electrical kind of smell. Some folks just associated it with the spooky atmosphere of the ride, but it was actually a by-product of mold, worn-out machinery, and old electrical wiring. And there was the occasional putrid smell of vomit covered with a layer of sawdust near the exits of some of the more violent rides.

To the locals, after a long desolate winter, summertime in Crystal Beach became a total sensory overload of all the unique things that made up the experience of living there: sights, sounds, smells, crowds, and parties, lots of parties.

To many residents, the amusement park represented their primary source of income. With several hundred jobs to fill each summer, the Crystal Beach Company was the major employer for a great number of year-round Beach residents. A lot of these employees went through hard times during the rest of the year, some having to survive on unemployment insurance and other public benefits, others just squeaking by to make ends meet until the next season's Memorial Day opening.

Seasonal poverty, along with year-round alcoholism, were realities to many villagers.

Park workers, like the residents, fell into different categories. There were "lifers," the people who worked at the park since they were young, some for decades. Roy Trider Sr., started on the Cyclone in 1941, then ran the Giant Coaster until 1983, a total of 42 years. He, along with a few others, were kept on in the maintenance and paint shops through the winter months to repair and maintain the rides for the next season. Sam Aquilina of Crystal Beach started in the park in 1960. He ran the Wild Mouse for years, then worked year-round on the Comet right up until the park closed in 1989.

Sam Aquilina, atop the Comet.   *The Comet in Hibernation.*

Photo: Rick Doan.   *Photo: Dale Roddick*

There were itinerant park employees, who didn't actually live in Crystal Beach, but would arrive in the village in May and find a place to stay at one of the boarding houses or cottages, while working one ride or another during the season. This was an annual practice from the early days back in the 1800s until the park closed. They were carnies. A lot of these seasonal employees worked for ride and concession contractors throughout the park, such as Conklin Shows, and would move on after Labour Day when the park would close, to work at the Canadian National Exhibition or the London Western Fair. Some of the rides went with them, but they would always be back again the following May. There were some very colourful characters who lived the carny life, and talked the carny talk, and many of them eventually settled in Crystal Beach.

Another group of park workers were the high school and college students who were lucky enough to land a summer job there. If you were really lucky, you landed a job as a lifeguard on the beach, and your bosses were Danny "Zack" Zaccagino and Van Hall, who became president of the Crystal Beach Company in 1973. Van was also a veteran U.S. combat fighter pilot, who still flew training missions with the Air National Guard out of Niagara Falls, New York. After a sly heads up from him the day before, sure enough there would be an F-4 Phantom buzzing right along Crystal Beach just above the water, the length of Abino Bay before climbing, then banking away and flying off into the distance.[35]

The park employed ride operators, electricians, plumbers, carpenters, mechanics, ticket sellers, concession workers, sucker-makers, cleaning crews, entertainers, ticket runners, game booth operators, clowns, private police officers, Pinkerton detectives, and security staff. The list is endless. In the summer, there were jobs for everyone in the village. There were so many jobs, in fact, that even American summer resident kids worked for the Crystal Beach Company, oblivious to the fact that it was illegal to work in Canada without an employment authorization. Most employees were paid via cash in pay envelopes anyway. The four-month period from May to September truly was the time to earn a dollar in Crystal Beach.

The population of Crystal Beach on any given day could perhaps be loosely categorized into four groups. First, the year-round permanent residents, mostly Canadians. They were definitely in the minority in the summertime in Crystal Beach. The earliest recorded population figures in 1921 listed 298 year-round residents of the village, yet by 1961 this figure had increased to just under two thousand year-round residents, with twenty-five thousand summer residents.[36]

Year-round residents either worked at the park, or at one of its spin-off businesses. Others were employed out of town in Fort Erie, Niagara Falls, or St. Catharines. Tourism and its spin-offs were the one and only industry within Crystal Beach. Many also worked for

American summer residents who required upkeep on their summer homes and cottages.

There were the summer residents. Mostly Americans, this group would swell the local population up to twenty-five thousand people or more each summer. Some had quaint little family cottages passed down through the years, which mixed in well with the year-round residences in the core area of the Beach. Locals readily accepted them into the mix and many lifelong friendships, and even marriages came out of this integration of Canadians and Americans each summer. A few old-timers had derogatory names for the Americans such as "Hot Dog Eaters" or "Yankees," but in general the Americans were welcomed each year by the "Canucks."

A lot of American summer residents had huge beach front homes along Erie Road and out into the Point Abino hills. Originally, many of these large, beautiful homes were owned by prominent Western New York families from very old Buffalo money. The appropriately-named Rich family of Buffalo, the Weigels, who owned Iroquois Breweries in Buffalo, several U.S. Congressmen, and many prominent Buffalo political figures all owned summer homes in the Crystal Beach area. Tenants of the Rebstocks at Bay Beach throughout sixty-odd years included many prominent Western New York businessmen, attorneys, FBI Agents, the Erie County Sheriff, as well as many other blue collar Buffalo families, who came to enjoy their little piece of summer paradise.

There were also seasonal or weekly renters, who may have stayed for a summer, a week or two, or even just a weekend, enjoying both the park and the beach. Fraternities, sororities, and college kids comprised the majority of this segment of the summer population. They were there to enjoy the beach and to party.

It was from within this group that the infamous cottage "pay parties" emerged. The cottagers would declare a party for a given day, then charge a flat "donation" fee at the entrance, giving the partygoers "free" beer once inside the fence. It was a way around obtaining a liquor licence to sell alcohol, which was basically a Crystal Beach tradition. There became so many cottage parties that eventually a schedule had to be drawn up for the events throughout the summer. Even the police would obtain a copy of the schedule and attend, just to make sure no one took alcohol outside of the temporary snow fencing containing the chaos, and that everything was shut down by eleven p.m. It was a uniquely Crystal Beach phenomenon.

There were some permanent residents who loved the pay parties, and there were also those who despised the noise and free-flowing booze enjoyed by the young partygoers. Many of the summer residents and seasonal or weekly renters would give their cottages clever, even obscene names, following a long-standing Crystal Beach tradition dating back to the 1890s.

A recent informal poll conducted in a Crystal Beach social media group revealed almost sixty separate cottage names within Crystal Beach during the 60s, 70s, and 80s, many of them participants on the pay-party schedule. Some of the popular cottage names of the later days around Crystal Beach were Wasted Acres, F.U.B.A.R., Magnificent Seven, and L.A.G.N.A.F. (Use your imagination for the last one). There were many others just as witty, some unprintable, as morality in Crystal Beach always ran the gamut of interpretations throughout the decades.

The naming of cottages is actually an old tradition in Crystal Beach, and goes back much further than the 60s and 70s. It was likely handed down through generations of American summer residents who had family summer places. Many newcomers to Crystal Beach are continuing to embrace the cottage-naming tradition today within the village. In the park's early days, before the Peace Bridge, many visitors stayed in Crystal Beach for longer than just the day. There were some hotels, but rooming and boarding houses were abundant throughout the village. When a rooming or boarding house became very successful, they simply started calling it a hotel, as the licence requirements in those days to conduct a lodging business were rather loose.

Summer vacationers, tourists, itinerant park employees, even day visitors who missed the last boat back to Buffalo, all needed places to stay. Most of the boarding houses and cottages which ringed the Queens Circle and the concentric roads around it in the core of the village had creative and exotic names, much like their successors in the 60s.

A 1927 Fire Plan map reveals many cottage and boarding house names, some dating as early as 1909. On the Queens Circle were the Martinell (owned by former police and fire chief Martin Strauch and his wife, Nellie), the Shepard, the Austin, the Bernstein's Queen Circle Inn, and the Iroquois. Moving outwards from the Circle, cottages started outnumbering boarding houses.

Cottage names were the Cloverleaf, Lincoln Cottage, the Maple Leaf, the Emerson, the Grand Jury, Glen Isle, the Albert, the Hollywood, Arcadia, the Delia, the Crescent, the Dorien, and the Malchen. Further out from the circle but still within the core of the village were the Rosebud, the Gertrude, the Parkview, the Buffalo, Villa Santa Barbara, Cook's Villa, Swiss Chateau, Orlando, the Cutley, the Ceck and the Augusta. Some of these original Crystal Beach houses and cottages are still standing today, over one hundred years later.

There were also many other places under the generic name "Boarding House" in the village core, bringing the total to well over fifty rooming houses just within the perimeter of Cambridge Road.[37] The Skerrett's Green Gables cabins, east of Ridgeway Road, provided lodging for thousands of Crystal Beach visitors and park workers over the years. The stories they could tell.

The tradition of naming cottages dates back even earlier to the early camper's tents and structures within the grove. In the summer of 1896, the following were just some of the names on various tents, cottages, and half-tent/half-cottages within the grove and on the southern Rebstock property: Juniper Cottage, occupied by Mr. and Mrs. William Dempster and Mr. and Mrs. Vosburg. The Embletons, and the Hickmans were in Dunraven, described as a "commodious tent." The Millers occupied Kenmore; Mr. and Mrs. Broad were in the Beehive; Mr. and Mrs. Arthur Hickman had a half-tent/half-cottage named Hickman's Roost; The Greens were in a cottage called The Pagoda, because it resembled one. Others with cottages within the grove were the E.C. Knights (the future Mayor of Buffalo), the Auerbachs, the

CRYSTAL BEACH: OUT OF THE PARK

Fells, the Bradishes, the Birds, and even the Rebstocks.[38] There's always been a place for a visitor to lay their head in Crystal Beach.

One singularly unique hotel establishment in Crystal Beach was the Hostess House, established in 1921 by the Buffalo Y.W.C.A. and the Traveller's Aid. The purpose of this establishment was to offer a safe place to stay for young ladies who had either missed the last boat back to Buffalo, or who may have been "duped" into missing the last boat to Buffalo by their male escorts, leaving them stranded in Crystal Beach with the scheming cad.

The Hostess House offered alternative and proper accommodation to ladies in this situation, rather than leaving them in the hands of their lecherous Lotharios. The house was supplied by park management, and the house manager's salary was also paid by the park company. The young ladies were allowed to stay the night and were provided with passage home the next morning on the first boat, as well as a letter from the Y.W.C.A. secretary who managed the hotel. The letter would explain the situation to "whomever it may concern," and that the woman had been provided with appropriate accommodations, thus preserving the young lady's reputation.[39]

There were visitors who came to Crystal Beach from Buffalo and around the Golden Horseshoe just for the day, to enjoy the beach or the park. At the end of the day they were gone, never even knowing that there was a village and a community surrounding all the fun.

The previously-mentioned Western New York company and community picnics which took place at Crystal Beach sometimes brought in up to twenty-five thousand people or more in a single day. They would hold activities in the stadium, go to the amusement park, and then leave on a bus at the end of the day, oblivious to the village. Black Rock Day, Kenmore Day, Westinghouse Day, Tonawanda Day, South Buffalo Day, and West Side Day were just some of the many group gatherings which constantly poured into the village every summer.

Depending on which category of resident or visitor one asked, a different description of Crystal Beach would be given by each one of them.

GARY POOLER

LOCAL LEGENDS AND OTHER STORIES

Growing up and living in Crystal Beach was a singularly unique experience in Canada. There were other popular beach towns in Ontario like Wasaga Beach, Sauble Beach, and Grand Bend, but none of them had the additional draw of a world-class American amusement park, and millions of American visitors.

It's difficult to describe Crystal Beach to someone who has never been there. Imagine growing up in Crystal Beach, where there was a giant free circus in the village every summer. Most of your friends were party-loving Americans. You hung out on one of Canada's best beaches, and there were hundreds of American girls walking around looking to meet Canadian boys.

There were bootleggers, where you could buy beer underage. There were giant pay-parties with live bands every Friday night. The list goes on. It was difficult to explain this place to your friends at university who grew up landlocked, miles from the border, where there was no amusement park, no beach, and no American friends. They didn't know whether to believe you or not, because they had never heard of a place like Crystal Beach. The few who came for a weekend visit to see for themselves became instant believers, often leaving with a serious hangover and a smile on their face.

As a kid, anything you wanted to do in the summer could easily be reached on your bike, or by walking or running. If you weren't hanging out at the park, the beach was the place to be. Easily reachable by foot for most cottagers, the beach would be packed seven days a week during the village's peak years. In addition to the narrow, close streets, there were also several narrow pedestrian walkways dating back to the village's origins, connecting one ring road with the next one out. The original pedestrian walkways Ulster Lane and Munster Lane still exist, and are still used today.

The layout of the roads and walkways were ideal for kids who liked to ride their bikes, or for folks who liked to walk to a friend's cottage for a visit. Being only one-square-mile, everything in the village could be explored or accessed in a single day. The village police department did not even have a cruiser until 1949. There was always sand along the shoulders of the roads near the beach, which added a relaxed, comfortable feeling to the village.

One of the many summer oddities in the Beach in the early 60s was a flagpole sitter named Skip Teal, who would sit in a box atop a giant pole in the parking lot of the Savannah Restaurant, more recently known as Lino's. The ridge where Skip sat in his flagpole box served as the gateway down into Crystal Beach, and thousands of visitors would drive by, hoping that Skip would wave down at them. It was one of those quirky things that made Crystal Beach what it was.

Skip, the Flagpole Sitter, 1950s.

Photo: Paul Kassay

In 1953, a twenty-five-year-old bylaw was resurrected by village council, and was enforced by Corporal Legate of the Ontario Provincial Police in regards to swimwear and modesty in public. The bylaw decreed that swim suits could only be worn within the village for swimming and only between the hours of five a.m. and ten p.m. While walking to and from the beach however, bathers had to wear a robe or coat with sleeves, covering the body in a decent manner. At least ten summonses were issued under the resurrected bylaw.

An elderly woman expressed her disgust with the immodesty being displayed before the bylaw went into effect by stating, "Look at that bulging, hairy man, now I know Darwin was right!" A teenage girl commented "The boys aren't complaining, but I can see what they mean about some of the older men."[40]

Probably one of the strangest stories to ever come out of Crystal Beach comes directly from the written word of George J. Rebstock, the founder's son, about a hermit named Hong Kong, who had dug himself a cave dwelling into the side of the sand dune near the Millington Skyway, which was the road going over the top of the Oak Ridge dune, leading down to the lake.

> About this time [early 1900s] there was an interesting character, a hermit who appeared on the scene, none other than Hong Kong who lived in a cave in the hill near what is the Millington Skyway. He and his dog would go about the area asking for food. When cottages were built and curious people started looking into his cave, he left for parts unknown.[41]

It is not mentioned in the account whether Hong Kong the cave hermit had a lake-view cave, or if he was in a cheaper north-view cave. It is very frustrating to accept that no amount of research or investigation will ever reveal the true identity of the Crystal Beach cave hermit, Hong Kong. Perhaps it is best that he was only a hermit, rather than a clown.

One particularly interesting Crystal Beach resident, photographer Harry Woolever, saw an opportunity with so many people coming into the village just for the day, and wanting to leave with a souvenir photo of their experience. He developed a one-hour photo development and drying system, and eventually sold the patent for this invention to the Eastman-Kodak company.

CRYSTAL BEACH: OUT OF THE PARK

There was also a mysterious old man who ran a magic shop on Erie Road and dressed all in black like an undertaker, seldom speaking. He had a Boris Karloff kind of air about him. Kids would go there to buy practical jokes like itching powder and stink bombs. Teenagers would buy skull rings, fake switchblades and cheap jewellery, like I.D. bracelets, which would inevitably end up on the wrist of an American girl at some point during the summer.

To one Crystal Beach youngster who frequented the dimly lit magic shop with the black curtains, this man represented the absolute epitome of all that was dark and frightening in the world of sorcery and magic, even though he was probably just a regular guy who simply knew how to create an atmosphere. It was rumoured that he was once an entertainer, possibly in vaudeville, but there is no way to confirm this now. Like Hong Kong the Cave Hermit, he too will remain part of the local folklore.

Another Crystal Beach resident with a colourful but little-known past was Cyril Vaughan Bell, known locally as "Cy." Born in Peterborough in 1904, Cy Bell started Commercial Signs of Canada in Toronto with his brother, Eugene. At the end of 1940, Parliament banned the importation of non-essentials, which included American comic books, so Cy and Eugene started Wow Comics to fill the void in the Canadian market. Under Bell Features and Publishing, they created several other comic book labels such as Dime Comics, featuring characters like Johnny Canuck, Canada's World War Two answer to Captain America.

Contrary to local myth, Cy Bell neither created or drew Johnny Canuck. He was the owner and publisher at Bell Features and he had many talented artists to do the artwork. The character Johnny Canuck dates back in Canadian history to 1869 as a character in political cartoons. Prior to joining the NHL in 1970, the Vancouver Canucks of the Western Hockey League used a lumberjack version of Johnny Canuck as their team logo.

Leo Bachle, one of Cy Bell's artists, reinvented the character as a Nazi-fighting, Hitler-punching Canadian super hero. Cy came up with the story lines and character development ideas.

Source: Library and Archives Canada, Leo Bachle

Other Canadian superheroes published by Bell Features were Nelvana of the North, Speed Savage, Thunderfist, and the Penguin. At its peak, Bell Features was publishing one hundred thousand comic books a week and employed sixty artists.[42]

Cyrus Bell moved to Crystal Beach in the 1950s and opened a small rooming house. In the mid-60s he went back into the sign painting business in a small shop on Erie Road near Elmwood, which he ran until he passed away in the 1970s. Cy was a well-liked and popular figure in Crystal Beach, and some of his sign-work still exists around the village and the Town of Fort Erie.

Another former Crystal Beach resident and Ridgeway-Crystal Beach High School student, Frank Kelly Freas, was a cover artist for Mad Magazine in the 1950's and 60's. He drew many of the Alfred E. Neuman cover illustrations, and eventually became known as the dean of science fiction artists.

Unrelated to Cyrus Bell, the Bell, Book & Candle was a Beat Generation-style coffee house located at the foot of the Millington Skyway, going over the hill towards the lake. It was a genuine beatnik place, and poets, artists, and folk singers hung out there. It was run by

CRYSTAL BEACH: OUT OF THE PARK

an artistic lady named Ruth Swayze. Some of the top performers from the Buffalo and Toronto folk scenes would regularly perform there.

Around 1964, after his family had moved to Buffalo, German-Canadian John Kay would hang out at the Bell, Book & Candle in Crystal Beach, where a girl that he was fond of was working. He would also often play there. This was just prior to him founding one of the greatest rock bands in history, Steppenwolf, and then co-writing the hit song "Magic Carpet Ride" in 1968 with Steppenwolf bassist Rushton Moreve.

Curiously, kitty-corner to the coffee house where he would play was the actual Magic Carpet Ride in the amusement park. It had the words "Magic Carpet Ride" painted in giant letters across the side of the building facing Ridgeway Road, which led to and from the coffee house. It's completely reasonable to assume that the title of the song was somehow embedded into John Kay's subconscious from passing by a sign reading "Magic Carpet Ride" multiple times (in the 60s, no less). Kay has never acknowledged the song's connection to Crystal Beach, but he has said that he may have smoked a joint or two while writing the lyrics. Perhaps a case of cryptomnesia, or simply an eerie coincidence, adding to Crystal Beach's allure and history.

John Kay did return to Crystal Beach once more, when he and Steppenwolf played a concert at the Crystal Ballroom on June 6, 1987. One has to wonder if he still remembered the Bell, Book & Candle from when he was a young man pursuing the young beatnik girl.

There have always been local stories, legends, and rumours about mobsters being connected to Crystal Beach for decades. These stories have been passed down and told for generations, but difficult to prove through research. Clandestine mob activity tends to not get documented in the historic records or the media.

What can be confirmed is that Stefano "Steve" Magaddino, a charter member of "The Commission", and head of the Buffalo crime family responsible for Buffalo, Hamilton and Toronto, once dated a Crystal Beach girl, and was a regular visitor to the village.[43] Steve "The Undertaker" Magaddino allegedly held meetings with other organized crime figures from around the Golden Horseshoe at two particular establishments within the village. He was associated with two local business owners, and also an unidentified bookie from the Crystal Beach area. This is confirmed by a declassified FBI surveillance report from 1964.[44] Both the Canadian and American authorities attempted to recruit two other local gentlemen associated with these establishments to act as informants against Magaddino, but they were unsuccessful in their recruitment efforts.[45] Crystal Beach was not a good place to have a part-time job as a confidential police informant.

There is also a story from a reputable, but very private, businessman in Crystal Beach, who managed many of the boarded-up summer homes for Buffalo families during the winter months. There is no plausible reason for him to have invented this story.

It was just after the famous November 14, 1957 FBI raid on the first Organized Crime Summit in Apalachin, New York that this businessman's father received a call from a Buffalo family connected to a well-known Jewish mobster from the Buffalo area. They requested that their summer residence in Bay Beach be opened up, and for the heat and water to be turned on. It was extremely rare for any of the summer residents to open up their summer places in mid-November. The reason given was that several gentlemen would be staying there for a couple of weeks.

Sure enough, as he and his father were preparing the cottage for habitation, several large sedans with New York licence plates rolled up, and several impeccably-dressed gentlemen took up temporary residence in the place. As they were leaving, the businessman and his father were told by these gentlemen, in no uncertain terms, that "they hadn't seen a thing."[46]

Perhaps the gentlemen were some of the fifty or so attendees at the Apalachin conference who had managed to escape into the woods surrounding the Barbara estate when the FBI raided it. Although the FBI arrested sixty people at Apalachin, and established for the first time the existence of a national organized crime syndicate in the United States, many of the attendees ran through the woods, and scattered far and wide to lay low for a while. It is, after all, only a three-hour drive from Apalachin to Crystal Beach. The "Apalachin Mobsters" story lives on in the category of "local folklore known to be absolutely true." It is often conflated with the fact that a Buffalo family named Lansky once owned a summer home on Rosewood Ave., however, no connection to Meyer Lansky, the notorious New York mobster, has ever been *officially* established in either instance.

Other notorious connections to Crystal Beach are convicted sex offender Harvey Weinstein, and convicted murderer Fred Tokars.

While attending college in Buffalo, Weinstein had found great success promoting concerts with Harvey & Corkey Productions, years before Miramax and Hollywood. He now sits in a prison cell, disgraced and powerless. The Weinsteins owned a cottage in Bay Beach on Cherryhill Circle.

The Tokars family of Amherst, N.Y. also had a summer place in Bay Beach on Erie Road. Their son, Frederick Tokars, was convicted of orchestrating the high-profile murder of his wife in Atlanta in 1992. His evil deeds are featured on the Discovery Channel's *The FBI Files*. Local stories and legends like these add to the off-beat, and sometimes dark history of Crystal Beach.

In the 1970s, local businessman and former village councillor Ted Kassay attempted to turn Crystal Beach into a Bavarian-themed village. Building facades were retro-fitted with Bavarian-style frontages. An annual Alps Festival was held, with Bavarian bed races, and a three-legged race to every pub in the village, where each competitor had to chug a beer before heading to the next stop in the race. There was even an unofficial attempt to re-name the village "Krystaldorf" (German for Crystal Village). The Bavarian Village theme in the middle of summer never caught on. Mr. Kassay put his heart and soul into restoring vitality back into Crystal Beach when it needed it but his efforts, unfortunately, fell short of his dreams.

One longstanding Crystal Beach tradition takes place on the Labour Day weekend, in the form of the End of Summer Parade, which is a simulated funeral procession for "Old Man Summer." Vehicles are decorated, some with their witty cottage names on them, then a parade ensues through the streets of the village, like a regular funeral cortege, only happier. The last vehicle in the parade carries a casket containing a dummy or mannequin dressed up as the deceased Old Man Summer.

In the old days, the event would culminate with the casket being set on fire, then set adrift out onto the lake. Sometime in the early 1950s, however, this was changed to a backyard bonfire at a selected cottage in order to cremate Old Man Summer. This came about after some residents became concerned about the burning casket polluting the water. The End of Summer Parade in Crystal Beach still adds to the eclectic vibe of the village, even today.

In the winter, the village would be almost completely deserted, with nothing to do for many of the young people. There were lots of boarded-up cottages and businesses for bored local youths to "explore" the inside of. One could even venture into the "closed" dormant amusement park, as it was left totally accessible throughout the winter with minimal security fencing.

Some kids would try to climb to the top of the Comet before being chased out by the winter watchman, Norm, who carried a pellet gun with him, and didn't hesitate to use it. Drinking and bootlegging were also popular winter pastimes to combat the boredom of the long off-season, and the loss of income from the park being closed. Everyone in town looked forward to the next May 24th weekend, but even more so to the American Memorial Day the following weekend, when the good weather, the excitement, and the American friends would return.

In February, you could be exploring giant ice caves along the lakeshore or playing hockey on top of the frozen water that you were swimming in only six months earlier. There were hockey games so big and wide that you would sometimes have to chase the puck for half a mile if you didn't stop a hard slap shot. There was also ice-fishing and ice-harvesting, which many people did simply for a source of winter income. Some, like the Teal family, harvested ice on a commercial scale. Crews would cut the ice out of the surface of the frozen lake, then wrap it in burlap and insulate it with saw dust. It would be stored in the Teal's Ice House on Cambridge Road, and would last long enough to supply the area with ice throughout the entire summer.

CRYSTAL BEACH: OUT OF THE PARK

Teal's Ice House provided year-round employment for many villagers over the years, and many locals welcomed winter, hoping the lake would freeze over.

Six months later, in the very same place you had been playing in ice caves, you could be working a summer job sitting on a lifeguard tower in eighty-degree heat, or just lying on a towel on the warm sand listening to the Beach Boys on WKBW.

In the winter, you could get frostbite on your toes playing down at the lakeshore, while in the summer, the white sand of the beach could get so hot your feet would burn. It was two completely different existences, transforming once May rolled around. This annual re-awakening of Crystal Beach happened every summer for over one hundred years, and it was a beautiful and exciting yearly metamorphosis.

1960s Crystal Beach postcard.

Photo: Gord Counsell

American flags would go up, far outnumbering Canadian flags throughout the village. In 1915, a Mr. Christie wrote to the Attorney General of Ontario to complain about the over-abundance of American flags on display throughout the village, and the noticeable absence of Canadian flags. The Attorney General responded that the matter is not one to be remedied by criminal law, but that it merely showed "ignorance" on the part of park management.[47]

People with the unique Western New York accent would again fill the grocery stores, the bars, and the beach. Canadians would jokingly mock their American friends' accents, while the Americans would do the same, laughing every time their Canadian hosts would say the words "eh?" or "about." In Crystal Beach, it was totally normal for the Fourth of July to be celebrated with more excitement than Canada Day. It makes sense, since the local Canadian population was outnumbered by Americans ten to one every summer. It is an annual Fourth of July tradition in Crystal Beach for residents of all types to gather around Abino Bay to watch the incredible displays of fireworks and bonfires along the lakeshore, like the old Grand Illumination in Cottage City.

Every summer, New York licence plates far outnumbered Ontario plates. Many cross-border summer romances would blossom, most of them literally May to September romances. When Labour Day rolled around and the park closed, the American girlfriends and boyfriends had to go home.

Still others met the love of their life at Crystal Beach. Many of them married and raised families that enjoyed both sides of the border. Some Americans immigrated to Canada, and moved to Crystal Beach permanently. Except perhaps for those communities in Maine that have the Canada/U.S. border running through the middle of town, it would be difficult to find a greater or closer co-mingling of Canadians and Americans in one small community anywhere else in Canada.

The community still has many lasting legacies of these meetings. Dual citizenship (Canadian/American) is still quite common in the Crystal Beach and surrounding areas as a result of this longtime summer friendship between people from two countries and cultures. The phrase "U.S. Landed" is a uniquely used—yet completely unofficial—phrase used in the area to describe one's border-crossing status. Technically it means "I am a U.S. Citizen, but I am a Permanent Resident (what used to be called a Landed Immigrant) of Canada." It is unlikely used so frequently anywhere else along the nine thousand-kilometre Canada-U.S. border.

CRYSTAL BEACH: OUT OF THE PARK

Because it is only ten miles from Buffalo, and straight across Lake Erie, the only television stations that the people in Crystal Beach could get prior to cable and satellite, were the local Buffalo stations, channels 2 (NBC), 4 (CBS), and 7 (ABC). With a good set of rabbit ears, you could get channel 11 out of Hamilton, or a snowy hockey game on the CBC. That was it. American influence all year round.

During the park's heyday, if a complete stranger was randomly plunked into the middle of this annual scenario, they would assume that they were at a carnival in a midwestern American town, yet they would be in Canada. Both the Buffalo Canoe Club and the Buffalo Yacht Club established stations in Canada, just west of Crystal Beach, across Abino Bay.

The amusement park changed hands several times throughout the years, but it has always been under the ownership and control of American businessmen, with the exception of Rudy Bonifacio. This was reflected in their promotional style and also throughout the village itself. Often overlooked in the history books is this one-hundred-year annual "Americanization" of the little village of Crystal Beach, Ontario. The financial, social, and cultural effects that the Americans had on the entire Bertie Township area was, and always will be, a blessing to the community. It is also another reason why Crystal Beach was one of the most unique communities in all of Canada to grow up and live in.

Today, where the historic amusement park once stood, there is a private gated community of quaint Cape Cod-style beach houses called the Crystal Beach Yacht and Tennis Club. The inner village still remains nearly unchanged in its layout and atmosphere, but many tasteful renovations and new builds have taken place. Once described as a combination camp meeting ground, Chautauqua Assembly, and continuous circus, it all started on the beautiful lakefront stretch of John E. Rebstock's farm in 1887.[48]

GARY POOLER

John E. Rebstock, late 1930s.

Source: Courtesy Tim Rebstock

John Rebstock passed away at close to ninety years of age in March of 1941, having laid the foundation for both the village and the park's one-hundred-year-run as one of North America's top summer destinations. Many residents feel that the founder of Crystal Beach should be commemorated in the middle of the Queens Circle, which he designed over 130 years ago. His name is referenced within the text of a plaque commemorating the amusement park at Ridgeway and Erie Roads. However, there is no stone, plaque, statue, or monument dedicated solely to honouring the founder of Crystal Beach, John Evangelist Rebstock.

Chapter Two:
The Prize Fighters

Over 160 years ago, when the illegal prizefights were being staged in the Point Abino sand hills, the point was uninhabited and undeveloped. The Civil War had yet to happen. Crystal Beach's beautiful white sand had yet to capture the imagination and heart of founder John E. Rebstock some forty years later, as he would have been just a toddler back in Buffalo when the fights were taking place.

There was no village yet, nor an amusement park. There were no houses or residents on Point Abino. The Point Abino Sand Company had not yet started mining the majestic dunes for sand to be shipped across the lake to Buffalo for use in construction. The Point Abino Lighthouse, today a National Historic Site, was still sixty years into the future. Abraham Lincoln was only just contemplating his upcoming run for the White House in 1860.

Point Abino juts out into Lake Erie two miles west of Crystal Beach, and forms a beautiful protected inlet known as Abino Bay. The point itself was just an isolated spit of marshy Carolinian forest, surrounded by towering sand hills, some reaching as high as two hundred feet. Crystal Beach would take root four decades later on the opposite side of Abino Bay.

Despite its isolation and difficulty to get to, thousands of people still managed to get there to witness several prizefights up in the hills, both for the entertainment and the betting. According to township records, the entire point was owned during the prizefighting days by Washington M. Sloan, Esquire.[1] Sloan became the reeve of Bertie Township in 1862. It is lost to history as to whether the honourable Mr. Sloan was aware that such brazen illegal activity had been taking place on his property out on Point Abino.

In 1857, the year of the famous Bradley-Rankin fight, the easiest and most practical way for thousands of people to get to Point Abino from Buffalo was to come across Lake Erie from Buffalo via steamer boat. As there was no landing pier yet, passengers would be brought ashore via punts and canoes upon their arrival. It was extremely isolated and there was only one primitive dead-end road which only went partway onto the point. This made it difficult to get to, especially for thousands of horse-drawn carriages.

Point Abino.

Photo: Author

From Buffalo, Point Abino is only twelve miles away on a direct line across the lake. Coming via land, it is closer to twenty miles. In addition, one had to cross the Niagara River by ferry at Black Rock to Fort Erie, then take the "turnpike," as it was called in those days, across the treacherous countryside to Point Abino. It can reasonably be assumed that the crowds at these events consisted primarily of rabid American fight fans who had arrived via boat.

In addition to the isolated location, the fights themselves took place high up in the dunes, which today are still a Point Abino landmark. Prizefighting was illegal on both sides of the border at the time, but law enforcement was much scarcer on the Canadian side. An isolated location like Point Abino was ideal. Towering hills covered in trees, with little bowl-shaped hollows of sand forming natural amphitheatres, all hidden amongst the foliage at the top. It was the perfect location for thousands of people to secretly attend a clandestine event.

One of the most celebrated bouts to take place in Point Abino was between Domenick Bradley and Samuel S. Rankin on August 1, 1857. It was an epic 152-round (some news reports say 157) bare-knuckle marathon between the two Irishmen from Philadelphia.

Rankin, a heavyweight, is described as being a tavern owner at Broad and Rose streets in Philadelphia, and weighed in at 190 pounds. Bradley, also a heavyweight, would normally weigh in between 210 and 220 pounds. For this bout, however, he agreed to make weight for the fight and came in right at 190 pounds also, matching up with Rankin. This was the first and only (at that time) heavyweight match where one of the contestants had to make weight.[2]

The crowd in the hills that day was estimated between four and six thousand people, the majority of whom had arrived by boat.[3] Many steamers and smaller boats were hired out of Buffalo by the spectators. Canoes, punts, and dinghies helped ferry people to the shore once arriving in Abino Bay. Bradley crossed the lake on the steamer *Globe*, while Rankin arrived on the *Britain*. New York Governor John King was there, and his attendance is celebrated in the lyrics of the Saugerties Bard's 1857 song, "Bradley & Rankin's Prizefight For $1,000 A Side," the song sheet for which would become quite famous itself.

The media at the time occasionally mistakenly spelled Abino "Albino," and would also erroneously describe Point Abino as being an island in the lake.

For the Bradley-Rankin bout, Isaiah Smith of Buffalo was chosen as referee.[4] The fight itself was reportedly uneventful, even boring by some accounts. Famous English pugilist "Izzy" Lazarus, briefly a resident of Buffalo, was in the crowd that day and stated that he almost fell asleep.[5] According to the Saugerties Bard's song about the event, another famous New Yorker was also in attendance that day. Old Bill Tovee, a popular New York prizefighting legend, would perform the announcing duties in Point Abino, as he did at hundreds of prizefights in New York City.

The fight started at four-fifteen p.m. in a hastily-built ring, and the most remarkable thing about the match was that it lasted 152 rounds. Bradley knocked Rankin down in almost every round, while never once leaving his own feet throughout the entire fight. At one point, around the 126th round, a local "deputy sheriff" entered the ring and ordered the combatants to cease and desist with their illegal activity "in the name of the Queen." After a chorus of derogatory jeers and cat-calls from the crowd, he was picked up and passed out over the ropes and through the crowd, and the fight continued. Dominick Bradley was eventually declared the winner after two hours and fifty-eight minutes in the 152nd round.[6] Bear in mind, this was a bare-knuckle fight.

In the media after the bout, Bradley vehemently denied rumours that he had challenged any American or Irish Protestant to fight him. He claimed that he had not been in a church in over ten years, and that he scarcely knew what his own religion was. He stated that he had never brought any man's country or religion into question. Bradley, while having a large fan base of Irish-Americans, claimed that he fought only under the colours of the United States: the red, white, and blue.[7]

None of the people who had arrived for the fight via water that day, and then set foot on Canadian soil, had been legally cleared to enter the country by a customs official, and it was suggested that the matter be referred to the United States District Court for follow-up.[8] More than likely, the hapless, frustrated deputy sheriff who had been manhandled out of the ring was the individual making this suggestion. It would have been impossible for any of the spectators arriving by boat to report their arrival to a Customs House anyway, as it was sixteen miles away, at the ferry crossing in Fort Erie. It appears the powers that be at the time did not, or could not, proceed with any type of prosecutions for this unlawful gathering.

CRYSTAL BEACH: OUT OF THE PARK

The fight is immortalized in the aforementioned song "Bradley & Rankin's Fight for $1,000 a Side" written by Henry Sherman Backus, a travelling songwriter known far and wide as the Saugerties Bard. It is a remarkable piece of early American sports journalism and entertainment. The writer, his songs, and his travels are discussed in the next chapter.

Roughly two months prior to the Bradley-Rankin bout, another less-celebrated contest was fought in the Point Abino hills in June of 1857. It matched Harry Lazarus of New York, and Denny "The Dreadnaught" Horrigan from England. Harry Lazarus was the son of the famous bare-knuckle fighter, Israel "Izzy" Lazarus, who had emigrated to the United States in 1850 when it had been arranged for him to fight Owen Swift. Swift was reputed to have already killed three people in the ring, and Izzy also took a severe beating from him.[9]

Harry Lazarus was only twelve when he arrived with his father in the Five Points neighbourhood of New York City, and quickly adapted to the street gang way of life. In the book *Gangs of New York*, Herbert Asbury describes Harry Lazarus as "having fallen into the company of thieves and confidence men."[10]

At one time, Harry had been accused of killing a man in California, but he managed to escape back to New York while out on bail. He became the owner of a public liquor house known as the X-10-U-8 (Extenuate) on Houston Street in New York. He took part in various prize fights during the 1850s, including the bout against Denny Horrigan in Point Abino, then a subsequent re-match against Horrigan on Navy Island, both in 1857.

On June 10, 1857 in Point Abino, Lazarus and Horrigan, both lightweights, fought a bare-knuckle match for ninety-seven rounds in front of a betting crowd of two thousand spectators. Lazarus measured in at five-feet, four inches tall, and 112 pounds. Denny Horrigan measured in at five-feet, one-half-inch, and also 112 pounds. The stakes for the fight were $600 a side.

After 178 minutes, Lazarus was declared the winner. Horrigan immediately demanded a re-match, which was set for October 10 on

Navy Island in the middle of the Niagara River, three miles south of the brink of the Horseshoe Falls.

In the weeks leading up to their October re-match, both Lazarus and Horrigan trained in the Buffalo area. Lazarus was trained by George Leese at a place called Craig's, seven miles outside of Buffalo. Horrigan trained at Bart Scott's, five miles outside of Buffalo.

Horrigan and his party were transported to the island by the steamer *Arrow*. The crowd was said to be larger than their first match in Point Abino, which would make it well over two thousand people. The stakes were set at $500 per side. The match went so long that the final few rounds had to be fought by candlelight. After 128 rounds and three hours of fighting, the match was declared a draw and the stakes were returned to each side.[11]

Harry Lazarus and Denny Horrigan fought once more, in New York City in 1861, with Lazarus once again emerging the victor. It seems that these two did not like each other. Harry Lazarus joined the U.S. Army during the American Civil War, obtaining the rank of captain and receiving an honourable discharge.[12]

After the war, Harry resumed his saloon-keeping activities at the X-10-U-8 in New York. On January 2, 1865, Harry Lazarus was murdered, stabbed in the neck during a dispute over some stolen property. His killer was Barney Friery, a local troublemaker who owned an establishment next door to the X-10-U-8. Friery was convicted and hanged, his public execution taking place at "The Tombs" in New York City.[13]

There were several other prizefights in the Point Abino hills and surrounding area on the Canadian side of Lake Erie, all because of its secluded location. Navy Island and Long Point were also very conducive to holding a secretive, illegal gathering of thousands of people. There are no sketches or photos of the Point Abino fights, but the illustration of the Heenan-Morrissey match below in Long Point is likely very similar to the scene in Point Abino.

CRYSTAL BEACH: OUT OF THE PARK

The Great Prizefight between Heenan and Morrisey, Long Point, Ontario, 1858.

Source: Library of Congress

"Australian" James Kelly of New York fought Edward "Ned" Price of Boston in the Point Abino hills on October 5, 1859. This fight took place in front of approximately one thousand spectators.[14] John Heenan, a combatant from the famous bout which had taken place on Long Point a year earlier in October, 1858, acted as a corner man for Price in Point Abino. Kelly had in his corner Harry Gribbin, who had previously fought in the Bertie Township area himself in November, 1857.

John C. Heenan lithograph, 1863.

Photo: Frederick William Nicholls, source: Library of Congress

In the 1858 Long Point bout, John Heenan, also known as the Benicia Boy, fought John Morrisey, an Irishman out of New York. Morrisey was an enforcer for Tammany Hall in New York City, and later a member of the U.S. Congress. Morrisey, who won the Long Point bout with an eleventh-round knockout, was a prominent player in the Five Points *Gangs of New York* saga. He once fought, and lost, to the Bowery Boy's Bill Poole, who was portrayed (as Bill Cutting) by Daniel Day Lewis in the movie version of *Gangs of New York*.

There were delays to the start of the October, 1859 Kelly-Price bout, one of which was raised by Price's corner over the sharpness of Kelly's spikes. The referee ruled that they had to be filed down to the correct sharpness. It is unclear how Price's corner came to the conclusion that Kelly's spikes were too sharp, short of someone having been stepped on. This indicates that the "ring" these prizefights were conducted in, was actually just a set of ropes, or some sort of barrier to contain the fighters, set up directly on a flat area of the bare ground, and that there was no actual canvas ring as we think of it today. Hence, the need for spikes.

Thomas O'Donnell of New York was appointed as referee. Ned Price was declared the victor after twelve rounds, with Kelly suffering "dangerous injuries" according to his physician. Upon returning to the ferry landing on the American shore, the entire Buffalo police force was waiting to arrest all parties involved in the illegal prizefight, spectators and combatants.[15]

Regarding Kelly's aforementioned cornerman Harry Gribbin and his previous bout in Bertie Township, he was once scheduled to fight Irishman Joe Coburn of New York in the Point Abino hills on November 18, 1857, but it didn't quite turn out that way.

Gribbin, a Brooklyn bar owner, and Coburn would battle for a purse of $500 a side. A steamer had been hired by both parties for transport from Buffalo to Point Abino, ten miles across the lake. However, at the last minute, the ship's captain deemed the lake too rough to cross and would not sail.

It was decided that the parties involved would cross by land, taking the ferry across the Niagara River at Black Rock, then horse-drawn carriages from there to Point Abino. Many smaller boats, punts, and dinghies were hired out at great expense to those who were stubbornly still willing to take the chance at crossing the lake. However, their voyage to the fight in Point Abino would end up being for nothing, as the fighters would never make it there.

Reaching the Canadian side of the ferry crossing, the poor state of the roads dictated that the fight parties would not make Point Abino in time for the match to be concluded by nightfall. A council-of-war was held between both sides and a farm one hour (approximately five miles) from the border crossing, somewhere in Bertie Township, was located for the fight to take place.

A friendly farmer offered up his spacious orchard for the ring to be set up in. The location for the ring, protected from the wind by outbuildings, was chosen by George Humphreys, and a referee from Buffalo was selected.

It would be difficult to determine where this fight actually took place and who the farmer was, other than through local family history. Coburn weighed in at 145 pounds, Gribbin tipped the scales at 147. It was reported that Gribbin had been delayed getting to Buffalo in the weeks prior, and had therefore gained four pounds, forcing him to overtrain going into the fight in order to make weight. The contest began at exactly 1:10 p.m. and Coburn was declared the victor after twenty-one rounds.[16]

The intrepid Point Abino spectators who braved crossing the lake in hired boats may have missed the excitement of the fight, but the friendly farmer, his family, and his friends and neighbours, were all no doubt thoroughly entertained.

Although it didn't actually take place in Crystal Beach, another rather curious fight took place close by on Navy Island, where Lazarus and Horrigan had fought their re-match in October, 1857. On Sunday, September 16, 1888, a prizefight between two female contestants took inside an abandoned barn on the island.

Mrs. Hattie Leslie, twenty, wife of John Leslie of Buffalo, measured six-feet tall, and weighed in at 168 pounds. She was a theatre performer, a wrestler, and a boxer who sometimes worked the American vaudeville circuit, doing sparring exhibits with her husband, John. The *Scranton Republican* stated, "She says she is twenty, but she looks twenty years older."[17]

Her opponent, Irishwoman Alice Leary, was trained by Jack Kehoe of Bradford, Pennsylvania and Curley Hughes of Buffalo. Miss Leary also measured six-feet tall, and weighed in at 148 pounds. A purse of $250 was put up by twenty-five Buffalo businessmen, with the winner taking all. Both fighters spent the night before the fight at the McComb Hotel on Grand Island. They were transported by steamer to Navy Island, arriving at 7:10 a.m.

The fight took place inside an old barn, as it was raining that day. The media at the time found it necessary to describe the two women's outfits. Mrs. Leslie wore white tights, and a sleeveless wrapper. Miss Leary in black tights, wine-coloured trunks, and white wrapper.

Both contestants wore thin leather fingerless gloves, lined with a thin layer of felt. Leslie's second was George La Blanche, a former U.S. Marine, while Billy Baker acted as second to Miss Leary.

Hattie Leslie dominated the fight from start to finish, and was declared the winner by knockout in the seventh round. When the parties involved in the contest returned to the ferry landing in Buffalo, Leslie, Leary, and Baker were all arrested and charged with prizefighting. George La Blanche, the former Marine, absconded back to New York.[18]

Hattie Leslie.

Source: National Police Gazette, 1888

Crystal Beach: Out of the Park

After Crystal Beach was purchased by John E. Rebstock in 1887, and the amusements of the midway gained in popularity in the early 1890s, the attention of the people of Bertie Township and Western New York turned to less brutal forms of leisure and entertainment.

In addition, wealthy Canadians and Americans started purchasing large tracts of land on Point Abino to build summer homes on. There was also a sand-mining operation that had started, exporting the sand for construction use across the lake in Buffalo.

The prizefights were simply squeezed out of the hills, which were becoming less and less hidden and isolated. The original Crystal Beach athletic field, then the stadium, gradually became the new venues for athletic competition in the area. In such open and legal public places, prizefighting as entertainment in the Crystal Beach area fell by the wayside.

There were some very colourful characters who graced the sand hills of Point Abino, many of whom could easily be the subject of an interesting book in their own right. Five Points gang members and Tammany Hall enforcers aside, perhaps the most colourful character to grace the Point Abino hills was not a prizefighter at all, but an eccentric travelling minstrel whose story is told in the next chapter.

Chapter Three:
The Saugerties Bard

The historic prize fights that took place in the mid-1800s at Point Abino, Navy Island, and Long Point, Ontario, were widely covered by many major newspapers of the time across the United States. Besides the newspaper coverage, tales of these epic battles were also spread far and wide via ballads and songs printed on song sheets, also known as broadsides.

A broadside was a one or two-sided printed sheet of paper which the writer would then sell to anyone who wished to catch up on current events of local or national importance. Broadsides of that time would be like today's social media. It was how many people learned the latest news and songs of the day. Many of these were posted in public places for all to read, while others were sold by travelling entertainers singing the latest news.

These minstrels and songwriters would report on major events by creating rhyming narratives, sung to the tune of a popular song of the day, and have copies printed. They made their living selling their songs and broadsides for a few pennies per copy wherever they went. It was an entertaining way to read—or sing—about local and national news. A travelling musical newspaper, if you will.

As detailed in the previous chapter, one of the more widely-circulated sports songs of its day is the tale of the epic 152-round bare-knuckle prizefight between Domenick Bradley and Samuel Rankin, in the Point Abino hills on August 1, 1857, across the bay from Crystal Beach. Sports writers from far and wide were present, as was an eccentric travelling minstrel who went by the name Saugerties Bard.

This particular song sheet was printed as a broadside by J. Andrews of 38 Chatham Street in New York City shortly after the event. It was written in a first-person narrative style, the songwriter evidently an eyewitness to the epic battle. The writer suggests it be sung to the tune of an old air called "Old Virginia's Shore."

It is a fascinating piece of sports journalism history, and the writer of the song has long been a mysterious figure in local historic groups in addition to his hometown in the Hudson Valley area of New York State. The song "Bradley & Rankin's Prize Fight For $1,000 a Side" was published in dozens of newspapers across the U.S. and Canada immediately after the event in 1857, and also many times since. This 160-year-old document exists in the public domain, along with other song sheets from the Saugerties Bard's career, in the U.S. Library of Congress and can be seen in finer resolution at www.loc.gov.

Source: Library of Congress

Crystal Beach: Out of the Park

The text of this song sheet is transcribed here:

Bradley & Rankin's Prizefight for $1000 a Side.
Ye sporting men give ear to song, that dwell both far and near,
Of the awful fight in Canada, you shortly now shall hear.
In round the first these pugilists made a noble fine display,
But a stinger Bradley sent that made Rankin on bumbo lay.

Chorus:
I'll carry you back to Abino Point,
Where Bradley and Rankins fought,
Two pugilists of great renown,
And science men well taught.

The rounds they fought were many, boys, one hundred
and fifty-two,
Two fifty-eight these heroes fought, and knock-downs were
not few,
Old Bill Tovee too was there, and many miles did go.
Just ask the boys who saw the fight, and they'll tell you that
is so.

I'll carry you....chorus.

And Governor King was there likewise on a tour to
Niagara Falls,
A perfect trump, good race-horse stock, and to feed at
Abino calls.
A thousand things I might relate that happened on that day,
How the heroes fought, the blows they caught, and in the ring
did lay.

I'll carry you....chorus.

They puffed and blowed, the claret flowed, and thousands saw the fun,
That came in yachts, canoes and punts, to see the victory won,
In round the last they called to time, but Rankin was too slow,
Exhausted now the hero fell, unable to strike a blow.
With deafening shouts they Bradley cheered who did the victory win,
Who washed his face, then smoked his pipe, and pocketed the tin.

I'll carry you....chorus.

J. Andrews, Printer, 38 Chatham St., N. Y.

The author of the song is identified as "Saugerties Bard." It seemed an odd name for someone, as Saugerties was a place in New York State, and Bard simply meant a poet or minstrel. Research revealed that Saugerties Bard was not his real name, but in fact, a nickname which had been bestowed upon him in his hometown of Saugerties, New York.

The Saugerties Bard turned out to be a gentleman named Henry Sherman Backus, who was born in 1798 in the Hudson Valley of New York State, the year after President George Washington had left office. Backus' father was a War of 1812 casualty, killed in 1813 at Sackett's Harbor.[1]

Henry Backus settled in Saugerties, New York, where he was for a time, a schoolteacher. He could play the fiddle, the fife, the drums, and the bugle. He and his wife Eliza had five daughters, and they lived in the village of Saugerties. Tragically, they lost their youngest daughter, Sara Anne, at the age of one. The pain and anguish that Henry and Eliza must have experienced is unimaginable.

Fate, however, with its cruel randomness, was not finished with Henry Backus. While still in mourning over the death of his one-year-old daughter Sara, Henry's wife Eliza tragically passed away. Henry was suddenly a single parent in the throes of grief, supporting four children.

After Eliza passed away, tragedy and sorrow would once again visit upon Henry Backus. When he became unable to care for his remaining four daughters, they were taken from him by child welfare authorities to be raised in homes that could properly care for them. This poor man, in the space of a few years, had lost everything in life that had any meaning to him whatsoever.

Since humans first became socialized into familial units, people have lived with the fear of loss within their nuclear group. The expression "a parent's worst nightmare" exists for a very good reason, because that's exactly what it is. A nightmare. And Henry Sherman Backus had been cruelly plunged right into the middle of one. His infant daughter died, followed by his wife. Then, his only remaining connections to family and love were taken from him. It is no wonder that after this traumatic series of events, Henry Sherman Backus apparently lost his mind and went completely and utterly insane. He ended up in a lunatic asylum in Hudson, New York.[2]

Hudson Lunatic Asylum, 1841.

Source: Hudson Area Library

Upon his release from the asylum, Backus took to both drinking and religion with equal fervor, and wandered the Hudson Valley and the Catskills in an old beat-up, horse-drawn wagon. It was pulled by a worn-out nag of a horse, and he was followed around by a pack of stray dogs as he travelled about selling songs, spreading the news of the day.

His talent as a multi-instrumentalist was a perfect skill set for his new vocation. Adding to his other eccentricities, he also had a wooden peg-leg, exactly like the fictional pirates. In the Hudson Valley, he was just considered a harmless, yet extremely eccentric travelling minstrel by locals and others, far and wide. The story behind the peg-leg is probably a book unto itself.

He proceeded to completely detach himself from his previous reality. It could be argued that losing his entire family was just too much for him to bear, so he simply left this life behind, both mentally and physically. Henry Sherman Backus became a completely new person, re-inventing himself as the Saugerties Bard, bringing news to people far and wide to the tune of cheerful melodies. Yet, his bouncy songs were always themed in darkness and tragedy, both in subject matter and lyrics.

After what he had been through, perhaps his new persona was his only alternative to the madness that he feared would overcome him if he stayed in his previous reality. His preferred genre in his writings were murder and mayhem, but also riots, explosions, prizefights, and fires.[3]

The written physical descriptions of him, along with a pencil sketch of him by John Hughes Kerbert, bring to mind Professor Marvel from *The Wizard of Oz*, just slightly more unkempt . . . and a great deal more insane. Henry Backus became affectionately known as the Saugerties Bard throughout the Hudson Valley and well beyond.

Mr. John Hughes Kerbert, who lived in Saugerties, spoke to folklorist Louis Jones about Backus in 1941. At the time, Kerbert was eighty-seven years old and said that he remembered Backus who, according to him, was "rather short, stocky, well built, long grey hair and beard, grey suit, a "Grant Hat" and wooden leg." He even drew a sketch of Backus from memory.[4]

CRYSTAL BEACH: OUT OF THE PARK

1941 Sketch of Henry Backus, by John Hughes Kerbert.

THE SAUGERTIES BARD.

Source: Murder by Gaslight

The Saugerties Bard sold his songs, ballads, and broadsides across New York State, and even travelled as far as Canada, covering many notorious events. In his blog (gothamhistory.com), sports historian John Thorn, the official historian of Major League Baseball, wrote that Backus occasionally wandered into Canada. In his later years, the Bard lived in the heart of New York City, and was a frequenter of the Five Points area, covering the murder and mayhem that regularly took place there.

On August 1, 1857, he was in Point Abino, Ontario across the bay from Crystal Beach, to observe the Bradley-Rankin fight, then set it to cheery music. The crowd that day was estimated at four thousand people.[5] Other sources reported six thousand. That is a lot of song sheets one could sell.

It is intriguing to imagine this colourful, eccentric wandering minstrel up in the hills of Point Abino, witnessing the fight between Bradley and Rankin firsthand. The song certainly appears to be written from an eye-witness perspective, and appears to be a firsthand account. It is a beautiful piece of local history, sports journalism, and American folklore.

Three weeks previous to the Bradley-Rankin match-up, on July 4 and 5, the historic two-day fight (some called it a riot) between the Dead Rabbits gang and the Bowery Boys gang in Five Points, New York City, took place. It has been depicted in both the book and movie *Gangs of New York*. It was witnessed first-hand, and written about, by the Saugerties Bard. His song about the event's murder and mayhem is probably the most famous song sheet account written about the event, and it was widely published. This song sheet is also viewable in higher resolution through the Library of Congress.

Backus could very well have made enough money from his "Dead Rabbits Fight" song sheets to travel to Buffalo three weeks later and purchase fare for passage on one of the steamers, tugs, or punts which brought thousands of people across the lake to Point Abino to see the fight. This, of course, would mean that the Bard's rickety horse-drawn wagon and dogs more than likely could not make the trip across the lake. Being from the Hudson Valley, he could also very well have crossed by ferry along the St. Lawrence near Cornwall or Ogdensburg, or at Black Rock to Fort Erie, wagon and all. Perhaps he just simply took a train, however the story is so much better imagining the wagon, the horses, and the dogs.

Curiously, one of the participants in the Dead Rabbits-Bowery Boys fight in New York which the Bard had written about, Harry Lazarus, had also been in Point Abino only two months previous to the Bard's visit, when Lazarus fought Denny Horrigan in June, 1857.[6] The Lazarus-Horrigan bout was covered in the previous chapter. It is amazing how small a world it was, even at that time.

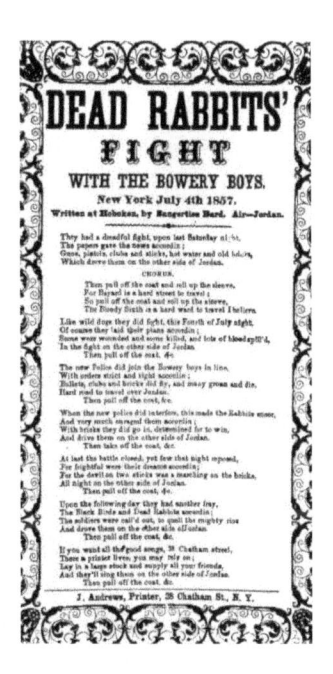

Source: Library of Congress

One of the Saugerties Bard's other famous works covering murder and mayhem, is his song about Hicks the Pirate, an 1850s New York thug named Albert W. Hicks. Historic tales vary, but one version is that Hicks was abducted and shanghaied onto an oyster ship, then got loose and proceeded to murder the entire crew. Hicks was captured when he tried to steer the sloop back into port, and crashed it into another boat.

The truth eventually came from Hicks himself, who admitted that he simply wanted to rob the captain of $800 that he knew was on board. The two other crew members were simply killed as witnesses, and thrown overboard along with the captain. He confessed his crimes as well as admitting to other acts of piracy involving murder.

Hicks was tried and found guilty. He was hung on July 13, 1860 in front of a crowd estimated at twenty thousand people.[7] The Bard wrote a cheerful and popular song about the hanging, appropriately titled "Hicks the Pirate." It, too, can be digitally viewed in the Library of Congress.

The Bard also wrote several accounts about the scandalous Bond Street Murder in New York, in which Dr. Harvey Burdell was murdered by his estranged lover, Emma Cunningham. She was subsequently acquitted of the crime after a hugely publicized trial.[8]

Another particularly gruesome event which Backus put to a cheery tune was the Thirteenth Street Murders in New York in 1858, wherein young Frank Gouldy, nineteen, butchered his entire family with a hatchet, then blew his own brains out with a three-barreled pistol.[9]

Backus most certainly did his best work putting the day's most horrific and sensational events to the backdrop of cheerful, airy tunes. Some other cheerful titles of the Bard were: "The Murdered Policeman," "The Murdered Pedlar," and "The Dying Californian."

The election of 1860, along with the onset of the Civil War soon became the main topics of interest in the American news. People gradually lost interest in the Bard's cheery songs about death and mayhem. They were getting enough of that sort of news coming from the battlefronts.

In 1861, penniless and in poor health, Henry Sherman Backus, the Saugerties Bard was arrested for vagrancy in Katsbaan, New York, near Saugerties. He was taken to the Kingston, New York jail and booked for vagrancy. He died in his cell on May 20, 1861.[10]

The legacy of Henry Sherman Backus, the Saugerties Bard, and his team of shaky horses will forever be woven into Crystal Beach history and folklore through his famous song about the Bradley and Rankin fight in the Point Abino hills for $1000 a side.

Chapter Four:
Crystal Beach Stadium

This chapter cannot possibly cover all of the events that took place at the Crystal Beach Stadium over sixty-plus years, but it will feature some of the more memorable and interesting ones.

When the original midway at Crystal Beach started gaining momentum in the late 1800s, a wide variety of quasi-athletic and daredevil displays appeared, alongside the rides, theatres, and sideshow amusements. Most were performed as exhibitions and stunts rather than actual sports competitions. There were high divers, acrobats, aerialists, parachutists, daredevils, and strong man demonstrations.

As the park grew, space for new rides was needed. The stunt performers with their apparatuses and high wires occupied a lot of land space along on the midway, which could otherwise be used for money-making rides and amusements.

The rides and attractions started outnumbering and out-earning the daredevil side shows, and the market for physical demonstrations evolved too. The athletic events were subsequently moved across Ridge (now Ridgeway) Road to an open field east of the park, and evolved into competitive and team sports like baseball, athletics meetings (track meets), as well as school and company field days. Although an earlier baseball diamond once existed on the west side of Ridge Road, a new diamond was laid out at the new location, which was referred to simply as the athletic field.[1]

In August of 1902, an athletic field day dubbed "Crystal Beach Day" was held for the employees of several Buffalo department stores such as AM & A's and Hengerer's. Events included a 100-yard dash, an 880-yard run, an obstacle course, a fat man's race, and a three-legged race followed by an evening vaudeville show.[2]

Crystal Beach Athletic Field, 1910, looking to the northwest.

Source: Toronto Public Library

A crude 440-yard running track was dug into the ground surrounding the playing field, and footraces of all distances became huge attractions to sports fans. The track was nothing more than a dirt oval, almost a foot lower than the grass level, with wooden curbs eventually marking the turns in later years. The home straight of the track ran just along the east side of Ridgeway Road in a north-south orientation, parallel to the Backety-Back Scenic Railway across the road. Originally there were no grand stands or stadium, the spectators would just line the field and the side of the track to watch the competitions.

In a photo of the start of the 1916 Buffalo Courier Derby, there appear to be at least three rows of elevated benches on an earthen berm, situated between the east side of the road and the home straight of the track, with spectators filling them. More bleachers were added as events gained popularity.

During the week of August 23, 1913, the godfather of a generations of great Finnish distance runners, Olympic Champion Hannes Kolehmainen, spent a week training on the Crystal Beach track for his upcoming world record attempt for the one-hour run. Large crowds attended just to watch him train. One of his workout sessions was a thirty-mile run on the dirt track, which is 120 laps. He was quite pleased with the facilities and the atmosphere in Crystal Beach. The promoters arranged for four of Buffalo's top distance runners to run against Kolehmainen in fifteen-minute relay legs each, in order to pace his world record attempt.[3]

On August 30, 1913, Kolehmainen finished just short of the world record in Crystal Beach, but he did manage to set a new American record for the one-hour run during his attempt.

Kolehmainen, the original "Flying Finn," won four Olympic gold medals and one silver, inspiring generations of world-class Finish distance runners, including Paavo Nurmi, Ville Ritola, Pekka Vasala, and Lasse Viren, all of whom became Olympic champions. During the early and mid-1900s, Finnish athletes dominated world distance running the same way that the East Africans do today.

Hannes Kolehmainen, after a thirty-mile run in the Crystal Beach Stadium in 1913.

Source: Buffalo Evening News

One of the earliest marquee events to be held at this location was the prestigious Buffalo Courier Derby, an annual five-mile road race sponsored by the owner and publisher of the *Buffalo Courier*, William J. "Fingy" Conners.

The first running of the Courier Derby was in 1916 and was held in conjunction with the annual Buffalo Central Y.M.C.A. athletic meet. Conners offered a diamond ring to the winner, a gold watch for second place, and a diamond stick pin for third. Conners always made a point of announcing to the media that the values of the various prizes were all below the allowable value limit for amateur prizes, as set by the U.S. Amateur Athletic Association (A.A.U.).[4] The annual Courier Derby was run for at least thirty-two years.

Crystal Beach athletic field, circa 1910s.

Source: Unknown

The race would start with two laps around the stadium track, indicating the existence of some semblance of a stadium at this time. The runners would then head out on to Ridge Road, which, at the time, was nothing more than a primitive, narrow roadway of compacted dirt, littered with rocks and stones.

On hot days, clouds of dust and exhaust fumes would be kicked up by the cars and carriages on the road travelling to and from Crystal Beach. There were no traffic control marshals to protect the competitors. They ran amongst and alongside automobiles and buggies on Ridge Road, which would be lined on both sides with Canadian residents and American tourists, cheering on the runners.[5]

The competitors raced out of the village northward to Nigh Road. The course would have been gruelling, with two quick hill climbs out of Crystal Beach over the ridge formed by the Crystal Beach Moraine. The first hill was at Rebstock Road, and then another at the glacial ridge, today known as Farr Avenue. The roads would have been dusty, rutted, and covered in rocks and stones. In the early days of the Courier Derby, Ridge Road ended at Nigh Road. It did not yet extend out to Garrison Road.

At the turn-around point at the Cauthard Farm at Nigh Road, an official "checker" was stationed in a parked automobile to ensure all runners ran the full distance. The athletes, each of whom wore a competitor's number on his chest, would have their number recorded by the checker as they raced around his car, then headed back towards Crystal Beach.

At the four-mile mark, there was another hill to climb, as the competitors again crested the ridge to go back down into the village. The racers would finish with two laps of the track in front of the spectators, running five miles in total.

The Courier Derby was run as a handicap race, with runners getting head starts of anywhere from thirty seconds to four minutes, based on how the officials assigned them. It made the event more spectator-friendly at the end as the time handicaps started equalizing. Most of the handicappers were caught and passed early on by the scratch runners, but some lasted well into the later stages of the race. As the stadium got closer, the faster scratch runners would gradually close the gap on those who had enjoyed their handicap. This format of racing produced many close and exciting finishes over the years.

The winner of the inaugural Courier Derby in 1916 was Carlo J. Nisita in 32 minutes, 2 seconds.[6] Nisita served in World War One with the U.S. intelligence services, and went on to become one of Buffalo's most prominent artists as a painter.

In 1919, several thousand sports fans were in attendance to see the finish of the Derby. Arthur Cotton crossed the line in 28 minutes, 40 seconds.[7] The crowds grew and so did the need for more seating capacity. In 1920, a mammoth new stadium was built at a cost of $74,000.[8]

The new grandstands would host thousands, who would come to see Olympians and world record holders compete in track and field events. The grandstand was typical of that era, with a long wooden structure running parallel to the home straight of the track, eight rows of wooden bench seats with backs. Spectators were shielded from the sun and rain by a sloped, protective roof which ran the length of the grandstands.

The grandstands at Crystal Beach Stadium.

Photo: Paul Kassay

Eventually, smaller north and east grandstands were added, increasing seating capacity to ten thousand. It was a beautiful yet functional structure, reminiscent of most small midwestern American grandstands or ball parks, and would have made an ideal location for a movie shoot. As with most things to do with the entertainment side of life in Crystal Beach, the promotions for the stadium events had a distinct hyperbolic American flair to them, with the main media coverage coming from the newspapers in Buffalo, New York.

CRYSTAL BEACH: OUT OF THE PARK

In 1925, Tommy Holden won the Derby in 28 minutes, 30 seconds, with a four-minute handicap. In the same race, Frank Wendling of Buffalo, the 1920 winner, recorded a scratch time of 26 minutes, 18 seconds, winning the silver trophy for fastest actual time. That is a remarkable time for five miles, even by current standards. His pace was 5 minutes, 15 seconds per mile. To put it in today's recognizable and popular road race perspective, at that pace Wendling would have passed the five-kilometre (5K) mark in 16 minutes, and 18 seconds, with two more miles still to run. Wendling represented the United States in the 1924 Olympic marathon in Paris.

The Courier Derby, as it came to be known, became one of the longest running, and most popular events in the history of Crystal Beach sports, with the prizes remaining the same throughout the years. Thousands of fans would pack the stadium, and hundreds more would line the roads to cheer on the runners. The Derby continued throughout the 1930s, and the 1940s.

In 1946, Don Munson, a twenty-five-year-old teacher from Amherst took the diamond ring in 26 minutes, 42 seconds, which would win many current local and regional road races.[9]

The Courier Derby was still going until at least 1948, when Art Henssler of Fredonia won the diamond ring in 27 minutes, 32 seconds, with a three-minute handicap.

Results of 1925 Courier Derby.

FIRST, SECOND, THIRD IN COURIER DERBY

Left to right, Tommy Holden, winner; Allan Clark, second, and Frank O'Connor. Clark is the 14-year-old boy who finished in the K. C. Marathon, going the full distance. O'Connor won the Courier Derby last year.

Order of Finish in Five-Mile Courier Derby

p.	Name and Club	Actual Time	Handicap	Elapsed Time
1.	T. Holden, unatt.	28:30 4-5	4 minutes	32:30 4-5
2.	A. Clark, St. Brigid's	28:52 1-5	4 minutes	32:52 1-5
3.	F. J. O'Connor, unatt.	26:47	1 minute, 30 seconds	27:47
4.	S. Leone, unatt.	26:51	1 minute, 30 seconds	28:21
5.	R. Graeber, C. Y. M. C. A.	29:28 2-5	4 minutes	33:28 2-5
6.	G. Kathlauen, Ashtabula	28:28 3-5	3 minutes	31:28 3-5
7.	C. Rhodes, Clarence Center	28:59	3 minutes, 30 seconds	32:29
8.	A. J. Macauley, unatt.	26:32	1 minute	27:32
9.	R. Zawierucha, Canisius College	29:46 1-5	3 minutes, 30 seconds	33:16 1-5
0.	F. E. Wendling, K. of C.	26:18	scratch	26:18
1.	A. Fager, Finnish-American A. C.	26:28 4-5	scratch	26:28 4-5
2.	I. Ruszczyk, Lincoln Playgrounds	30:12	3 minutes, 30 seconds	33:42
3.	S. Crofts, C. Y. M. C. A.	28:31	1 minute, 30 seconds	30:01
4.	G. Gressel, C. Y. M. C. A.	30:14	3 minutes	33:14
5.	E. Nolan, Guyro A. C.	31:19	4 minutes	35:19
6.	C. Hertel, Weed A. C.	29:59	2 minutes	31:59

Source: Buffalo Courier Express

CRYSTAL BEACH: OUT OF THE PARK

As far back as 1919, the Crystal Beach Stadium was also the long-time host to numerous Western New York School meets, in addition to the Erie Club's Buffalo Police Games. The Erie Club was an association supporting Buffalo Police athletic events.[10]

Early track race at Crystal Beach athletic field, circa 1910s.

Source: Unknown

The highlight of the Erie Club's annual meet was always the invitational events featuring track and field's elite stars of the day, including Olympians and world record holders. It became one of the prestige meets on the world-class invitational track tour.

In those days, amateur athletic status was strictly regulated and enforced by the U.S. Olympic Committee, headed by Avery Brundage, and track and field was probably the most scrutinized sport. Unlike today's superstars, track athletes of that era were paid nothing. Appearance fees, as we know them today, were absolutely forbidden. There were also no shoe contracts or sponsorship deals. Track athletes were expected to strictly adhere to the code of amateur athletics: To compete not for remuneration, but for the love of sport.

Touring athletes were only allowed travel expenses, accommodations, and meals, along with a per diem. By skipping meals, saving their per diem, and sharing accommodations, some of the busier amateur track athletes could actually make more money than they would back home, especially during the depression. Of course, this meager income was in addition to the occasional "plain unmarked envelope" which frequently changed hands between promoters and athletes or their agents at some of the more prestigious events.

Phil Edwards, 1928 Olympic Games.

Source: Canadian Sports Hall of Fame

From a Canadian perspective, one of the most celebrated competitors to grace the track at the Crystal Beach Stadium is undoubtedly Phil Edwards. Born in Guyana, Edwards attended New York University where he captained the men's track team. Later, he moved to Canada and attended McGill University. He competed for Canada in both the Olympic Games and the British Empire Games. Edwards won a Gold Medal in the 880 yards at the 1934 British Empire Games in London, becoming the first black athlete to win a medal in what is now known as the Commonwealth Games.

Edwards also won five Olympic bronze medals representing Canada in three separate Olympiads: 1928 in Amsterdam, 1932 in Los Angeles, and 1936 in Berlin. His Olympic medals were in the 400 metres, the 800 metres, and the 4 x 400 metre relay. Phil Edwards was the first African-Canadian to graduate from McGill's medical school. He joined the Canadian Armed Forces and attained the rank of Captain, and went on to become a prominent medical doctor specializing in tropical diseases. He was the first person to win the Lou Marsh Trophy as Canada's top athlete, and is a member of the Canadian Sports Hall of Fame.[11]

Phil Edwards competed at Crystal Beach on August 28, 1929, in a 600-yard exhibition sprint, setting a new stadium record of 1 minute, 9 seconds. At that pace (and continuing another 175 yards further) Edwards would have come very close to today's 800-metre world record.

On the same day that Phil Edwards competed in Crystal Beach, U.S. Olympic cyclist Iggy Gronkowski of Buffalo placed second in the one-mile bicycle sprint, then teamed up with Al Miller to win the four-mile team pursuit. At the time, there was a crude cycling track or pathway, semi-superimposed onto the running track. It was more egg-shaped, and may have been created to lessen wear and tear on the running track surface. The home straightaway and finish line in front of the grandstand, however, were shared by both the running and cycling tracks.

The winning time in the one-mile sprint was 2 minutes, 41 seconds, while the four-mile team pursuit was won by Gronkowski and Miller in 10 minutes, 40 seconds.[12] Ignatius "Iggy" Gronkowski is the grandfather of NFL players Dan, Chris, Glenn and Rob Gronkowski.

Crystal Beach Stadium, 1920. Overlapped running and cycling tracks.

Source: Canadian Postcard Company

Phil Edwards competed again at Crystal Beach on July 12, 1930. He was matched up against Harold Cutbill of Boston in the 880 yards at the Erie Club's Police Games.[13] That same week, in addition to the Scottish Highland Games competition, the Pierce Arrow Company of Buffalo company picnic at Crystal Beach drew a crowd of eighteen thousand people on Saturday July 26, 1930.[14]

On Dominion Day, 1931, Johnny Weissmuller, who became famous portraying Tarzan, gave a swimming and diving exhibition at Crystal Beach, but it is more likely that this event took place near the pier, as opposed to a swimming tank in the stadium. Johnny/Tarzan would demonstrate the different swimming strokes and talk about water safety, after which he would do a monologue and comic routine with Buddy Kruger.[15] Cheetah did not appear with him.

The 1930s can truly be called the Golden Age of high-end sports performance at the Crystal Beach Stadium. Three of the most notable competitors from that era, Olympic silver medalist and mile world record holder Glenn Cunningham, Eulace Peacock, America's top sprinter of 1935, and the great Jesse Owens, all made appearances there.

Before he became internationally famous by winning four gold medals at the 1936 Berlin Olympic Games, Jesse Owens was already considered America's greatest all-around track athlete. In 1935, even though he had set three world records within a forty-five-minute time span in Ann Arbour, Michigan, he was not having much success against one particular rival.

Owens was beaten several times by a Temple University student named Eulace Peacock leading up to their July 6th clash in Crystal Beach at the Erie Club's annual Police meet. The biggest loss that Jesse had suffered so far in 1935 had been to Peacock only two days earlier on July 4 in Lincoln, Nebraska. Peacock ran the 100 metres in 10.2 seconds to defeat Owens and 1936 Olympic silver medalist Ralph Metcalfe, for the U.S. National Championship. It was a pending world record at the time, but was later ruled to be slightly wind-assisted.

The track and field world was still not fully converted to metric distances from the Imperial system of yards. The 100 metres, being a marquee Olympic event, was one of the first events to switch from yards to metres (100 metres = 109 yards) in North America. The metric distance was in line with the international Olympic standard. Commonwealth countries initially stuck to the Imperial distances, but were gradually adapting to the new metric system. The 220, 440, and 880-yard races all followed suit in the following years, converting to 200, 400, and 800 metres.

The annual Erie Club's track and field meet or "carnival," as it was referred to in those days, was also called the Erie Club's Police Games, due to their association with the Buffalo Police Department. Held every summer for decades at the Crystal Beach Stadium, it was a day-long track meet, which culminated in the featured elite invitational events in the early evening.

The definite highlight on the bill for July 6, 1935 was the showdown between Jesse Owens and Eulace Peacock. Owens was most likely under enormous pressure to win, after having lost to Peacock only two days earlier in Lincoln. Every fan and sportswriter present that day likely expected, or even demanded, that Owens would redeem himself, and Peacock probably sensed that.

On Friday July 5, 1935, the day before the Crystal Beach race, Jesse and his fiancé Ruth Solomon decided to get married in Cleveland, where they lived at the time. They then spent the entire night dancing and celebrating with friends at a party thrown in their honour. Jesse then caught an early train to Buffalo the next morning, arriving in Crystal Beach the day of the race.

Since Eulace had arrived in Crystal Beach well before Owens, the *Buffalo Courier Express* photo of the two shaking hands, was more than likely taken either in the amusement park or in front of the Crystal Beach Stadium prior to, or after the race.[16] It also could very well have been taken at the Ontario Hotel on the day of the race, where Jesse and Eulace sat down with reporter Ray Ryan prior to their five-p.m. match-up. Owens and Peacock, who were good friends as well as rivals, spent time relaxing in the lounge of the Ontario Hotel at the corner of Erie and Derby Roads. They may have been sitting in what is now a store named Planks.

Eulace Peacock (left) and Jesse Owens (right) in Crystal Beach, 1935.

Source: Buffalo Courier Express

The July 7, 1935 article by Ryan from the *Courier Express* describes their friendly rivalry during their down time before the race. After some friendly small talk and discussion of the upcoming race, Jesse and Eulace strolled together down Erie Road to the stadium, to change and begin their warm-up routines.[17]

CRYSTAL BEACH: OUT OF THE PARK

Eulace and Jesse must have been exhausted, having raced at the National Championships only two days earlier, then both having endured long, overnight train rides. The Crystal Beach race itself featured only three competitors: Jesse Owens, Eulace Peacock, and a young college runner from Buffalo, Isaac Meadows of Michigan State.

Five thousand people were in the stands to witness the event. A special police detail was assigned to keep the crowds back from the track and the star athletes. The portrayal of the Owens-Peacock showdown at Crystal Beach in the movie *Race* is shot in a pouring rainstorm, likely for dramatic effect. It was very effective, but in fact, it was actually warm and sunny in Crystal Beach on the day Jesse and Eulace met. The two would actually compete in a driving rainstorm three days later in New York City.

The crowd at Crystal Beach was so excited to see the two stars in action, that Peacock and Owens agreed to also do an exhibition long jump "competition" after their 100-metre feature race. The air was filled with excitement and thick with tension as the three sprinters stretched and did striders up and down the home straight in front the main grandstands, still in their warm-up suits.

Young Isaac Meadows must have been beside himself warming up alongside the two track superstars. Being from Buffalo, his proud family no doubt packed the bleachers. This moment probably became one of the highlights in the Meadows family's history, passed down one generation to the next.

Owens and Peacock were likely wearing what they had competed in two days earlier in Nebraska: Owens in his scarlet Buckeyes track singlet with "OHIO" in white and silver letters across the front, and Peacock in his white Temple jersey, emblazoned with the Owl's crimson block letters. The wardrobe people from the movie *Race* seem to have believed the same.

Once out of their heavy cotton warm-ups, and after a few more practice starts and striders, the three athletes would be called to their marks by the starter. In those days starting blocks were neither used or allowed yet. Competitors would simply dig small holes with a trowel behind the starting line in which to place their feet, for something to apply force against at the sound of the starter's gun.

From today's perspective, standing on Ridgeway Road looking east at the new homes in the current Marz housing development, the competitors would have been running from left to right, or north to south. The actual finish line of this race would have been approximately one hundred metres north of where today's municipal sewage treatment plant now stands.

Owens got away first with a quick start, and held on to a slight lead. He and Peacock soon left the young Meadows behind. At the 75-yard mark, Peacock caught Owens. There was some apparent contact between the two as Peacock passed Owens, but race officials and both competitors shrugged it off after the race.

Peacock broke the tape in 10.5 seconds.[18] Eulace Peacock had once again vanquished the great Jesse Owens. His time is remarkable both for the era, and for the poor quality of the cinder, dirt, and sand-mix track at the Crystal Beach Stadium.

In addition to not having starting blocks, the track spikes worn by the athletes of that era were leather and much heavier. They had small steel anchoring plates in the forefoot to provide a solid base onto which the permanent inch-long metal spikes were welded. They probably weighed close to one pound each. Today's track spikes by comparison are made from synthetic materials and carbon fibre, and have removeable interchangeable spikes which can be adapted to whatever surface a runner may be competing on, usually a very fast rubberized surface.

A modern-day sprinter's shoe weighs in at a fraction of the spikes used in the 1930s. For example, Michael Johnson's famous gold Nike spikes from the 1996 Atlanta Olympics weighed just over three ounces each. Peacock's shoes in 1935 easily weighed five times that amount.

Taking the technology, the track surface, and the shoes into consideration, Peacock's 10.5 seconds in Crystal Beach would easily equate to a world-class time today.

What is unfortunate is that there are no known photographs of the Crystal Beach race, only descriptions and media reports. After the Crystal Beach meet, Ray Ryan of the *Courier Express* reported that a large after party was held at the Crystal Beach cottage of Detective Thomas F. Coyne of the Buffalo Police Department.[19] It is lost to history as to whether Jesse and Eulace attended the gathering.

Three days later in New York, Peacock defeated Owens again, running the 100 yards in 9.7 seconds, in the rainstorm portrayed in the movie as having happened in Crystal Beach.

Jesse Owens, of course, would have much greater success thirteen months later, when he would win four Olympic gold medals within the space of six historic days in Berlin, Germany.

The whole world would come to know the dramatic story of his Olympic performance in front of Adolph Hitler in Berlin in 1936.

Jesse Owens at the 1936 Olympic Games.

Source: commons.wikimedia.org

History and fate, however, had other plans for Eulace Peacock. Just prior to the 1936 U.S. Olympic Trials, he severely tore a hamstring muscle in his right leg, and was unable to make the 1936 Olympic team. World War Two cancelled the next two Olympics, and Eulace was never able to fully recover from the injury. He took up the Pentathlon, which then consisted of the 200-metre sprint, long jump, javelin, discus and 1500-metre run. He became U.S. National Champion six times, but was never again the pure sprinter that he once was. At one time also one of the world's greatest long-jumpers, Eulace Peacock just loved the sport of track and field, and simply wanted to experience the joy of competition, no matter what the level or the event. He competed into the 1940's before retiring.

Peacock joined the U.S. Coast Guard as a P.T. instructor, serving under Commander Jack Dempsey, the great heavyweight boxer.[20] He competed again at Crystal Beach on June 19, 1940, in front of a crowd of eight thousand fans at the Annual Erie Club's Police Games. He won the 100-yard dash in 9.8 seconds, from two yards behind the scratch position, and also captured the 220-yard dash in 23.2 seconds from five yards behind the scratch position.

In the 100, Peacock finished ahead of James Robinson of the Butler-Mitchell Boy's Club of Buffalo, Frank Walter, and Howard Cook of Rochester. At this same event, Robert Ballantyne of the Canadian Parachute Club, piloted by Raymond Chesney, made a spectacular parachute jump from only one thousand feet, landing on the stadium infield to the delight of thousands of spectators.[21]

Eulace Peacock (left) winning again at Crystal Beach, June 19, 1940.

Source: Buffalo Courier Express

CRYSTAL BEACH: OUT OF THE PARK

The story of Jesse and Eulace's epic rivalry is depicted in Stephen Hopkin's excellent 2016 movie, *Race*. In the scene showing their Crystal Beach encounter, the director pays a touching homage to Crystal Beach Park and the Cyclone roller coaster, as you can see the silhouette of a large coaster in the background of the shot as Jesse and Eulace shake hands. Eulace Peacock later opened a liquor store, living a quiet life as a family man. He passed away from Alzheimer's in 1996.[22]

2- WORLD CHAMPIONS -2
AT
CRYSTAL BEACH STADIUM
TOMORROW

| JOE LOUIS | GLENN CUNNINGHAM |
| WORLD'S GREATEST FIGHTER | WORLD'S FASTEST MILER |

Image: Buffalo Evening News

On August 20, 1938, heavyweight boxing champion Joe Louis appeared at the Crystal Beach Stadium. He was doing a celebrity meet-and-greet for the fans, promoting the events in the stadium that day. He would also present the trophy to the winner of the invitational Courier-Express Mile, which Glenn Cunningham would be running in.[23] Louis arrived in a large yellow Cadillac convertible, and wore a lime green suit and a large yellow hat. He was a huge hit with the fans and they flocked to see him, swarming him by the thousands.[24] He had to be escorted away to a secure area by the extra police detail that was on duty that day.

Cunningham, the former world record holder in the mile, had made several appearances at the stadium, and this night would be his final appearance in Crystal Beach. He was a fan favourite wherever he went, and would compete in the feature event that evening, the invitational mile. Although never as big a household name as Jesse Owens, Cunningham's story is every bit as compelling.

Cunningham had overcome crippling leg injuries suffered in a school house fire as a child, to become the world record holder in the mile and an Olympic silver medalist in the 1500 metres. He became an unlikely champion of the underdog, and a symbol of hope and inspiration for millions of Americans during the Great Depression.

When Glenn was growing up in Elkhart, Kansas, he loved to run. He ran everywhere. He would run through the pastures, racing the family cows. He would run beside his father's wagon, instead of riding with his siblings. He would challenge his older brother Floyd to race to school in the morning, then back home again in the afternoon.

One of his chores at the one-room school house that he attended with his siblings was to start the fire in the pot-bellied stove prior to their classmates and teacher arriving. On one particular day, when Glenn was eight and Floyd was thirteen, unbeknownst to them, someone had mistakenly put gasoline into the kerosene container that they used to get the morning fire started. The container exploded, igniting both the school and the boys' clothing into flames.

Others arrived at the school to find the school engulfed in flames and pulled the two brothers out of the inferno, both still on fire and horribly burned. Glenn's brother Floyd did not survive, dying at the family home after nine days of agony.

The lower half of Glenn's body suffered catastrophic tissue and skeletal damage, with large amounts of skin, muscle, and ligaments burned away.[25] The injuries were extensive, but contrary to the frequently-repeated myths popular with sports journalists, the transverse arch and toes of his left foot, although seriously damaged, were not burned away, as can be seen in a photo of him barefoot in 1934.[26]

CRYSTAL BEACH: OUT OF THE PARK

Glenn Cunningham, 1934.

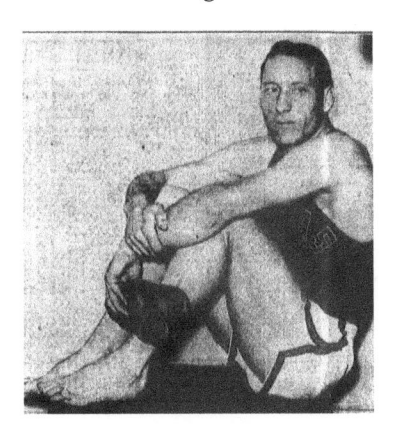

Source: Buffalo Evening News

Through the haze of semiconsciousness, young Glenn heard the doctor tell his mother that he would probably never walk again, and that amputation of his legs may even be necessary. Glenn begged his parents not to consent. He spent six weeks completely motionless in bed, then the better part of a year learning just to stand up and balance on his own. He used a wooden chair for balance at first, then a single crutch as he eventually forced himself to learn how to hobble, then walk. He didn't take his first step until fourteen months after the explosion.

His knees were unable to flex or extend at first, and his right leg was locked in a semi-bent position, making it slightly shorter than his left leg when Glenn did try to walk. Even as an eight-year-old, he summoned the sheer grit and determination to drive himself through the pain. He came from a family of tough dirt farmers from the Kansas prairies, who at one time lived in a tent and travelled in a covered wagon.

Eventually, when he was able to barely walk, he focused on one thing: he wanted to run again. It was an incredibly slow and agonizing process for a young boy to push himself through on sheer will and determination, but once he was able to run again, he never stopped. He ran everywhere.

He ran when he did his chores. He ran when he brought the cows in. He started running to school and back again every day. Once again, he was able to run beside his father's wagon.

For the rest of his life, his legs required daily massages and stretching exercises due to the tremendous amount of scar tissue in his extremities. Scars and open leg wounds stayed with him his entire life. So did the pain. The skin on his lower legs was mainly inflexible scar tissue, and was extremely prone to breaking open, and vulnerable to spike wounds from other runner's shoes. In the George R. Rebstock photo of Cunningham at the Crystal Beach Stadium from July, 1937, one can see that Cunningham still wore bandages on his scarred lower left leg from the burn injuries that happened some twenty years earlier.

Glenn went out for the track team in high school and in only his second year, he set a world scholastic record for the mile run of 4 minutes, 24.7 seconds. He then went on to a stellar career on the University of Kansas track team, winning the NCAA Championship in 1932. In 1934, he set a new world record in the mile and became hugely popular with sports fans across the United States. The fans knew his story, and at that time America rooted for underdogs.

Like Seabiscuit, boxer James Braddock, and other underdogs of that era, Glenn Cunningham gave millions of Americans a sense of hope during the Great Depression. He ran in the Olympic Games in 1932 and in 1936. In 1936 on the boat trip to the Berlin Olympic Games, he was chosen as "Most Popular Member" and Captain of the U.S. Track Team by his team mates. He and Jesse were roommates on the ship and became good friends.

CRYSTAL BEACH: OUT OF THE PARK

Glenn Cunningham at Crystal Beach Stadium, July, 1937. The other runner is from Buffalo Athletic Club. Northeast corner of the stadium track.

Photo: Courtesy George R. Rebstock

At Berlin, Cunningham won the silver medal in the 1500 metres, with Adolph Hitler in the stands as a spectator. Glenn Cunningham went on to serve in the U.S. Navy, acquire a Ph.D., and do speaking tours, motivating millions of people to overcome adversity in life.

He and his wife Ruth ran the huge Glenn Cunningham Youth Ranch in Nebraska for underprivileged and at-risk kids. Horsemanship and equine care were a big part of the curriculum there, as was discipline and spiritual exploration. Glenn and Ruth Cunningham positively affected over ten thousand young people's lives during their three decades of running the ranch.[27]

On July 21, 1934, Glenn Cunningham and Ralph Metcalfe, who would finish second to Jesse Owens in the historic Olympic 100-metre final in Berlin, both competed in the Erie Club meet at Crystal Beach. A crowd of eight thousand people watched Cunningham run a special three-quarter mile invitational race.[28] He defeated fellow U.S. Olympians Frank Crowley and Joe McCluskey in 3 minutes, 8 seconds.

In the same meet, Ralph Metcalfe defeated Ben Johnson (no relation to the 1988 Canadian Ben Johnson) and Ed Siegel in the 100-metre event.[29] The Ben Johnson that raced in Crystal Beach on that day went on to become one of the first African-American colonels in the United States Army.[30]

One month prior to this appearance at Crystal Beach, Cunningham had set a new world record in the mile of 4 minutes, 6.8 seconds in Princeton, New Jersey. Cunningham ran the mile even faster indoors, clocking 4 minutes, 4.4 seconds at Dartmouth in 1938, sixteen years *prior* to the four-minute mile barrier being realistically challenged and then broken by Roger Bannister.

August 20, 1938, the day Joe Louis was swarmed by fans as he was signing autographs, would be Cunningham's last appearance at Crystal Beach. He defeated Gene Venzke, Joe McCluskey and Don Lash in the feature *Courier Express* Invitational Mile. His time of 4 minutes, 19 seconds was attributed to it being a slow tactical race, and very poor track conditions.[31]

In 1939, eleven thousand people attended the annual Erie Club's Police Games track meet.[32] This was one of the largest crowds ever in the history of the Crystal Beach Stadium, but sadly, things were about to change.

After the golden era of Owens, Peacock, Cunningham and Edwards, events at the stadium were plentiful, but not nearly as well promoted. World War Two wiped out two Olympiads in the 1940s, and as a result track and field's popularity waned. Drawing the huge stars of the day became next to impossible. Amateur athletics played second fiddle to the war effort.

The Buffalo Olympic Club attempted to promote another footrace, a ten-miler from the foot of the Canadian end of the Peace Bridge, finishing at the Crystal Beach Stadium.[33] This event never caught on like the Courier Derby had, but legend has it that the trophy from this race is in the possession of someone in the local Buffalo running community.

CRYSTAL BEACH: OUT OF THE PARK

*Glenn Cunningham at Crystal Beach, 1938.
Police Chief Frank Reavley doing crowd control.*

Source: Buffalo Courier Express

After the lull in events during the war, meet promoters managed to attract world record holder and Olympic gold medallist Herb McKenley of Jamaica to compete at Crystal Beach in 1948, with him winning a 400-metre race in 48.1 seconds at the 57th Annual Buffalo Y.M.C.A. Meet.[34] McKenley's appearance in Crystal Beach was one of the last meets featuring elite, world-class competition.

The following thirteen Olympians, most of them medalists, appeared at the Crystal Beach Stadium over the years:

Americans Jesse Owens, Glenn Cunningham, Archie San Romani, Joe McCluskey, Frank Crowley, Gene Venzke, Frank Wendling, and Iggy Gronkowski. Canadians Phil Edwards, Bill Fritz, and Lawrence O'Connor. Dennis Shore of South Africa, Hannes Kolehmainen of Finland, and Herb McKenley of Jamaica.

In June 1950, Hollywood movie star Gloria Swanson appeared at the stadium to present trophies to the winners of several events that day. Ms. Swanson had been in Buffalo on a nation-wide promotional tour for her new movie *Sunset Boulevard*. The meet promoters scored quite a coup in securing her appearance that day.[35]

Gloria Swanson at Crystal Beach Stadium, 1950.

Source: Buffalo Courier Express

Another high-profile American visitor to the Crystal Beach Stadium was New York Governor and future Vice President of the United States, Nelson Rockefeller. He attended the Erie County Republican picnic on August 25 1962, drawing the largest ever one-day crowd at Crystal Beach at the time. The gathering would have been in the Crystal Beach Stadium, followed by a visit to the amusement park.[36]

In the following decades, there were low-level exhibition wrestling matches, with some of the wrestlers even making Crystal Beach their permanent home, adding to the village's unique and quirky make up. The crowds for the events of this era were nowhere near the size from the golden era. Crowds in the mere hundreds became the norm in the 50s and 60s.

As the quality of the events and the size of the crowds shrunk at the stadium, baseball and softball games became popular there, mostly between rival communities or companies. There was Midget Baseball—yes, baseball played by a travelling troupe of actual little people. Inappropriate today, but that's what it was called back then. There were also donkey baseball games, in which batters/baserunners were required to ride a donkey around the base paths as opposed to running. Even a horseshoe pit was installed for competitive and recreational use.

On September 8, 1957 two sections of the stadium containing seventy-four hundred seats were destroyed by a fire that started in the pony barn where hay was stored. Eighteen hundred seats were saved from burning, which gives an indication as to the capacity of the stadium. Fortunately, the ponies were saved and the flames did not spread across the street to the amusement park. The owners stated their plans to rebuild for the following season.[37]

After the fire, in the 60s and 70s large feature events did not return to the stadium. Sports and entertainment at the Crystal Beach Stadium had definitely jumped the shark by the 1970s. School field days, company and church summer picnics, and softball games became the norm. There was the odd wrestling exhibition or variety show, but the Crystal Beach Stadium had run its course. As the amusement park declined in attendance owing to, among other factors, new theme parks going up within driving distance of Buffalo, so did the number and quality of events at the stadium.

GARY POOLER

Crystal Beach Stadium in flames, 1957.

Photo: Courtesy Cathy Herbert

In its final years, the Stadium sat vacant, with nothing racing through it but the wind off of Lake Erie. Local teenagers used the deserted grandstand seats as a place to drink beer, smoke pot, and make out. Locals and visitors alike would just drive past it on their way to the Palmwood via the Millington Skyway, oblivious to its once-glorious past. It became a forgotten background structure that was always there, empty, until people just gradually stopped noticing it.

Crystal Beach Stadium south gate, abandoned, late 1980s.

Photo: Courtesy Cathy Herbert

CRYSTAL BEACH: OUT OF THE PARK

After the closure and sale of the Crystal Beach Amusement Park property, the Crystal Beach Stadium was eventually bulldozed from all memory to make way for real estate development in the early 1990s. Today, neo-traditional cottage-style houses sit along the home straight of the track where Jesse Owens, Eulace Peacock, Glenn Cunningham, and Phil Edwards once put on world-class athletic performances in front of thousands of cheering fans. Most of the current residents in these houses, however, have no idea that Jesse Owens and Eulace Peacock once raced through their backyards.

In the early 1970s, one Crystal Beach youth sought out the remnants of the stadium track on the advice of his track coach, who had told him the stories of the glory days of track and field at the stadium. Both the track and the infield were now simply used as a parking lot for the hundreds of cars and busses bringing visitors to the park.

All the young runner could find was a faded portion of the northeast turn, where Glenn Cunningham once stood in 1937 to have his picture taken by a young George R. Rebstock. A few cinders and dirt were all that was left of lane one, which had long been worn away by vehicle tires. The young man ran a few laps on the ghost of the once-legendary track, then ran home.

CHAPTER FIVE:
LAW AND DISORDER

Every small community has a historical scandal or notorious event that occasionally comes up in conversation amongst locals. The Crystal Beach Amusement Park and the Village of Crystal Beach are no different. They have both experienced their share of scandalous—and tragic—events over the years. One of these was the horrific death of twenty-three-year-old Amos Wiedrich of Buffalo on May 30, 1938. Wiedrich was thrown from his seat on the infamous Cyclone roller coaster onto the tracks below, then run over by the speeding coaster at fifty miles per hour. With the ride filled with horrified thrill-seekers, his head and feet were severed by the speeding cars at the point of impact. His torso was then dragged another two hundred feet along the track, grinding the cars to a halt.

Park representative Harry Hall and village police would testify that the solid lap bar was in the locked 'down' position when he got to the car after the accident. Other witnesses contradicted this, testifying that the bar had come loose. One witness stated that Wiedrich had his arms over his head as the ride reached the top of a banked turn.

Coroner James Stackhouse's jury ruled that the reasons for the young man exiting the car would never be known. A civil lawsuit filed against the Crystal Beach Company in Welland County Court was eventually settled with a payout to the Wiedrich family. Eight years later, the

Cyclone was torn down and replaced by the tamer, yet equally famous Comet in 1946.[1]

There have been other tales and misinformation about people dying on the Cyclone, but Amos Wiedrich was the only one. People may be ascribing other fatalities associated with the park as having happened on the Cyclone, simply due to its fearsome reputation.

In the park's very first fatality in 1910, 17-year-old Louise Koch of Buffalo died on the Backety-Back Scenic Railway when, for reasons unknown, she left her seat while in the tunnel section of the track and was killed. In the 1940s, an employee died of a heart attack while working on the Cyclone, but it was unrelated to the ride.

In 1975, a 26-year-old man from Stevensville was killed after falling, or climbing, out of his seat on the Comet, and in 1980, an electrician on the Comet was killed in a work place accident.

In May of 1956, an infamous fight or "race riot" as deemed by some in the media, took place between two large groups of American youths, allegedly one black and one white. Other news reports describe Italian and Hispanic youths being involved. Arguments and scuffles, which had begun in the amusement park, continued and escalated during the ten-mile return trip to Buffalo on the steamship *Canadiana*. This event has been a hot topic amongst Crystal Beach historians and sociologists for decades. Corporal Legate of the Provincial Police called it a race riot, while park management claimed it was nothing more than a fight between two groups of teenagers, and that it would never happen again. Depending on the media source one read, opinions were many and diverse.

The incident did, however, prompt the Ontario Provincial Police (OPP) to increase their detachment strength in Crystal Beach to twelve officers, including officers within the park. This was in addition to the park's own "special police," who were the only officers actually allowed on the boat under an unofficial international agreement.

While Crystal Beach Amusement Park was never segregated, from the beginning its clientele had been mostly Caucasian up until the early 1950s when the second Great Migration of African-Americans brought five million people to northern cities. African-Americans who settled in the Buffalo area in the 1950s became regular visitors to the park. Crystal Beach has always been a very open and welcoming community.

However, with such a rapid change in the racial demographic of the park's clientele, an incident like this, at that time, would certainly have caused many outside observers in the media and the public to draw conclusions that race played a role in the *Canadiana* fight. The park owners ensured that this type of occurrence would never happen again by permanently discontinuing the *Canadiana* service on Labour Day, 1956.[2]

These events all took place within the amusement park, and were covered by the local and Buffalo media. Park management had a great working relationship with the press. For good reason, reporters favoured the park as a news source, and these types of events were obviously preferable to the mundane daily events in the village itself. That all changed in 1951, when the darkest chapter in the Crystal Beach's history took place.

Police and political scandals from the 1940s and early 1950s, involving the village council, the police department, and the volunteer fire department, were raising the ire of many citizens. Some even suggested that these events led up to, and contributed to, a horrific murder within the village.

The Buffalo media descended on Crystal Beach to cover and sensationalize this event. The whole thing came to be referred to by locals as "the bootlegging scandal," which is a curious choice of words. One would think that it would have been referred to as "the murder scandal." It would lead to the demise of the Village of Crystal Beach Police Department.

One of the earliest references to an actual police officer serving in Crystal Beach is Officer William Gilchrist in 1895. His son, also named William Gilchrist, was described as a county constable.[3] It is unclear as to who exactly employed the elder Officer Gilchrist, as he was in Crystal Beach twelve years prior to the OPP even being formed, and twenty-four years prior to the village incorporating and forming their own police department.

Gilchrist could have been a provincial or county constable like his son, which were appointed positions that existed at that time wherever they were needed. He may have been appointed by the Bertie Township police magistrate. It's also entirely possible that Mr. Rebstock himself simply granted Gilchrist the title as a private police officer for the resort park.

In subsequent years, the amusement park owners would simply appoint their own "special police" and have them sworn in by a magistrate, with their area of responsibility being limited to within the park property. In June of 1949, Chief William Diamond, along with Constables Earl Schuett and Ernest Easto, were sworn in by Magistrate Hopkins to the Crystal Beach Park Police.[4]

There may have been a cost-sharing between the park and the village as the park police seem to have worn the exact same uniforms as the village police, other than their shoulder tabs. The park police were not armed, however, they were more than just security guards. In June of 1946, Crystal Beach Park Police Chief William Diamond was severely beaten by a Buffalo youth who had been causing a disturbance in the park.[5] He also assisted the village police and the OPP with several significant investigations over the years.

Private police within the amusement park are again referred to in 1956 after the *Canadiana* fight.[6] It appears that the concept of "private policing," at least within the Crystal Beach Amusement Park, was in existence long before it began being seriously discussed by North American communities in the latter part of the 20th century.

Officer Gilchrist (the elder) lived in one of the first cottages to be built in Crystal Beach, "The Rustic," which was on Derby Road near where Cambridge Road and Bea's Dry Goods would later stand. He obviously had the nickname "Old Gillie" because his son was also a police officer in the area.[7] It's just a guess, but his son likely had the nickname "Young Gillie."

In May of 1895, a self-styled "Strongman" named John Lacey arrived in the village looking for work, perhaps as a performer along the midway. He was described as over six feet tall and enormously built. When his plans to perform feats of strength on the midway

CRYSTAL BEACH: OUT OF THE PARK

didn't work out, he took on jobs around the area as a manual labourer. He was reputedly able to single-handedly lift fallen trees or huge construction beams when teams of other workers could not budge them.

On June 29th, 1895, as has happened with many other young men throughout the decades at Crystal Beach, John Lacey got drunk and obnoxious while at the beach. He began by harassing other beachgoers, then escalated to hooting and hollering as he chased them around, screaming threats. Lacey was described as a screaming, raging drunk on the warpath.*

Officer Gilchrist, along with his son William, the county constable, attended the beach and demanded that Lacey be quiet and settle down, to which Lacey responded by laughing and telling the two lawmen to run along.

The Gilchrists attempted to arrest him, but Lacey was in a mood for a fight. A huge donnybrook broke out, with other beachgoers jumping in to help the two officers subdue the crazed giant. After exhausting himself, Lacey was arrested and taken to Police Court in Ridgeway where he was fined fifteen dollars and warned by the Magistrate.

Lacey swore vengeance against the senior Gilchrist, threatening to spill his blood. Days later, after getting drunk once again, Lacey waited outside the Gilchrist residence, threatening and yelling at anyone who came near. Both Gilchrist men came out and confronted Lacey, who again was looking for a fight. He stole a whip from a nearby buggy and began howling insanely, hitting the elder Gilchrist with the handle portion.

Gilchrist Sr. told his son to go back inside and retrieve their revolvers. After injuring the elder Officer Gilchrist's leg, Lacey unsuccessfully tried to steal the buggy from its owner, eventually leaping off and running away. While on the lam as a fugitive, Lacey stole a revolver two days later from Ridgeway resident Thomas Kennedy. Lacey's wife said that he had told her he was going to kill the older Gilchrist.

---

* Author's note: I am positive that I saw John Lacey's great-great-grandson do the exact same thing one hot July afternoon in the early 1970s.

Working as a father-son detective team, the Gilchrists found that Lacey had fled to Buffalo, New York, and they contacted the police in that city. Lacey was located and arrested by the Buffalo Police and held for "extradition" which, in those days, simply meant that Constable Gilchrist (the son) travelled to Buffalo and retrieved a heavily-manacled Lacey from his Buffalo counterparts. Gilchrist simply replaced Lacey's American handcuffs with his Canadian handcuffs, and the 1895 extradition process was complete.

Upon his return to Canada, John Lacey was taken immediately to Welland County Court, and found guilty of assaulting a Queen's Officer, and for the theft of the revolver. He was given a one-year prison sentence, and was advised that when he finished serving that time, he would then be charged with threatening to kill Officer Gilchrist. Lacey, described in the media as the "Giant Terror of Crystal Beach," was taken away to serve his year in prison.[8]

The senior Gilchrist apparently earned his salary keeping law and order in the village. On September 5, 1897, John E. Rebstock, the founder of Crystal Beach, reported a burglary of one hundred cigars and three dollars in change from a cigar store in Crystal Beach to the Buffalo Police. Rebstock believed that the culprits were on the excursion boat *Dove* and were headed back to Buffalo.

Two boat workers, Samuel Victory and Adolph Garold were arrested by Buffalo police upon their arrival at the Buffalo ferry landing. They were returned to Crystal Beach and, along with a third man who was arrested in Crystal Beach by Constable Gilchrist, charged with larceny and burglary and remanded into custody at Welland County Jail. All of the property was recovered.[9]

On Saturday September 26, 1899, Constable Gilchrist—whose title had changed from Officer to Constable at some point—teamed up with the summer cottagers on "the hill" to extinguish a fire which he believed was an act of arson started by a group of tramps who had recently infested the village and set up a hobo camp.[10]

As Crystal Beach became more popular, the summer population would swell to numbers which were unmanageable by whatever law enforcement service was assigned to Crystal Beach at the time. This was most likely a police magistrate from Bertie Township, or county and provincial appointees, like the Gilchrists.

In 1898, Crystal Beach was designated a Police Village, its first official status as a place. As a result of the summer population explosions, the OPP created its first "summer only" detachment in 1915, when a Provincial Constable Jackson was assigned to Crystal Beach for three months.[11]

Upon incorporation as a Village in 1921, council created its own small police department of one chief constable (William Scott), and two constables.[12] These officers were unarmed and received little, if any, formal training—unless they had come from an established police service.

For most of the year, the operation of the Crystal Beach Police Department was reminiscent of what Andy Taylor and Barney Fife had in the town of Mayberry. But only for eight months. Things were manageable for them throughout the winter. A few cottage break-ins, the odd domestic call on weekends, but generally it was very quiet.

However, from May until Labour Day was a very different story within the square mile that comprised the tiny village of Crystal Beach. The village would also hire unarmed auxiliary constables for the summer months to help with the crowds. These summer-only officers would also have received little, if any, training.

At various times throughout their years in the Beach, the OPP had offices at the municipal hall, and also at a small detachment in the office buildings just within the amusement park property. Their primary responsibility was the village, but they would help maintain the peace within the park, and assist the park police. Prior to incorporation, the police offices were in this building, where Justice of the Peace Ed Buck would preside over Crystal Beach's police court. In the very early days, old Officer Gilchrist worked out of the magistrate's office beside Harry Emerson's Supply House.

The original Crystal Beach village jail was in a small stone building just northeast off of Queens Circle at the corner of Loomis and Shannon Roads, which is now a private residence. The current resident has the original iron jail cell door mounted on a shed as a decoration.

For decades, summers in Crystal Beach meant an influx of cottagers, beachgoers, and weekend partiers, mostly from across the border in Western New York. During the park's golden days, the local population in the winter hovered anywhere from three hundred to two thousand people. The summer population, however, has been estimated as high as thirty thousand or more during the village's heyday. This was in addition to the thousands of day visitors who came to Crystal Beach solely for the amusement park.

On some corporate picnic days at Crystal Beach, twenty-five thousand people or more would disembark from the busses bringing them there for the day from Buffalo. In the early days, and up until the 1956 youth fight, the steamer *Canadiana* would deliver another three thousand people or more per trip, back and forth from Buffalo, sometimes up to ten trips per day, all summer long.

On a given summer day, there could be well over fifty thousand people within the village boundary. Most enjoyed the amusements within the confines of the park, but some did venture out into the streets of the village, and over to the beach, seeking other forms of entertainment.

Throughout the years, noise, traffic, parties, and the "informal" sale of liquor and beer were generally tolerated by the local population, many of whom relied on their seasonal jobs at the amusement park and its "spin-offs" for their livelihood.

By the mid-1940s, however, more than a few year-round residents and members of council were growing tired of the parties, noise, and bootlegging taking place within the village.

In the early 1950s, widespread bootlegging, drug use, and immorality were alleged by an angry citizen's group who called themselves the vigilance committee. The anti-vice "vigilantes" were spearheaded in part by Reverend D. R. Pilkey of the People's United Church.

There was also the perception that some council members and village police force officers were not taking law enforcement seriously enough, even looking the other way in regards to the widespread illicit activities. [13]

CRYSTAL BEACH: OUT OF THE PARK

Looking back as early as the mid-1920s during the Ontario Temperance Act, there had been provincial inquiries into bootlegging and "drunken revelries" in the Crystal Beach area. These allegations were always, as expected, vehemently denied by the village and the management of Crystal Beach Amusement Park.[14] That sort of reputation would be bad for business all around.

The illegal sale of alcohol was a huge money maker for bootleggers in Crystal Beach. Back home in New York State, American visitors were used to walking into any corner or liquor store at any hour to buy beer or liquor. However, once arriving in Crystal Beach, Ontario, there was only one beer store two miles away in Ridgeway, and it closed at six p.m. If one ran out of booze in Crystal Beach, there weren't many legal options as to where and how to re-supply.

Another thing driving the Crystal Beach bootlegging market at that time was the fact that under Ontario law, liquor could only be sold in hotels and taverns between noon and six p.m., and from eight p.m. to midnight.[15] This void in the supply and demand chain—i.e., way more demand than supply—within the village became apparent to several opportunistic individuals, so they took to meeting the "spiritual" needs of the summer population through bootlegging. Crystal Beach folks have always been very industrious at making a quick buck.

Bootlegging is defined as the illegal supply and sale of goods that are subject to government taxation or prohibition. This dirty little secret of Crystal Beach that most of the locals were aware of, and its subsequent fallout involving a murder, became what is known in local folklore as the Crystal Beach "bootlegging scandal."

As things reached the boiling point in the late 40s and early 50s, claims that crime was running rampant increased. There were allegations of young people committing indecent and immoral acts, while drugs and booze flowed at the cottage parties. Mass depravity was said to be taking over the village. Some members of village council complained that police laxity was contributing to the alleged lawlessness.[16] The police countered that a lack of resources, and limitations imposed by council on the use of the police vehicle, prevented adequate enforcement.

One has to bear in mind that in addition to the year-round and seasonal summer residents, most of the weekly or weekend cottage renters were twenty-something college students from everywhere, but predominantly Western New York and beyond. It was a summer beach town where everyone would let their hair down. What else would one expect?

Complaints of rowdyism in Crystal Beach went back decades. As far back as 1925, citizen's outlandish complaints of drunken debauchery and sex orgies had been directed to the village police. Raids were sometimes conducted as a result of such complaints, often resulting in little evidence, and only minor charges.

One such raid took place in 1925 at a cottage named "Restmore" on Lincoln Road, and also at two other locations. This operation illustrates the discrepancy between the seriousness of the complaints coming in, versus what was ultimately found to be taking place. Complaints had been received about drunkenness, prostitution, and indecency at all three of the locations.

Crystal Beach Police Chief George Pinkerton and two provincial police officers, W. B. Elliot and George Wilkinson conducted raids at all three cottages in the early hours of June 24, 1925. All that was found at "Restmore" was one case of whiskey and a small amount of beer. The occupants were all peacefully playing cards, and only one arrest was made. George Carr, a former motorcycle patrolman on the Ridgeway to Fort Erie line, was taken into custody for supplying the whiskey. The other two places had nothing illegal going on inside, the occupants all fast asleep.[17]

The possibility exists that since the local police were involved in the raids, these places may have been tipped off beforehand. If so, it would help explain both the sudden firing of Police Chief George Pinkerton and the hiring of his replacement, World War One hero and Victoria Cross recipient Michael O'Leary, at the very next village council meeting in June of 1925.

Chief Michael O'Leary's story, also involving scandal and controversy, is covered in the next chapter. George Pinkerton would soon be back as chief constable by September of 1925, after O'Leary's subsequent dismissal. It would not be easy going for him, though.

On June 20, 1927 during the arrest of three men, Pinkerton, who was unarmed, was shot at by one of them, the bullet grazing his head.[18] At this point in time, the village police were neither armed, nor did they have a police vehicle. That luxury would not even be discussed until 1948. Until then, the police walked, or drove their own vehicles if necessary.

Edward Clunie was appointed chief constable of the Crystal Beach Police Department in the spring of 1929. He was a Scotsman who had immigrated to Canada two years earlier with his family. A World War One veteran who had a portion of his lower jaw shot off during combat at Flanders, he was well-liked by the village citizens, and had a reputation as a law-and-order police chief.

Unfortunately, on June 19, 1929, while intoxicated, Chief Clunie drove his vehicle into a refreshment stand along the midway at Crystal Beach Amusement Park. He was arrested and charged with driving while intoxicated. OPP Constable Fred Coulthard pleaded with the judge for leniency for the shell-shocked war veteran, but Judge Massie sentenced Clunie to seven days in jail, and he was dismissed from his position with the police department.[19]

Clunie's replacement as Crystal Beach police chief was Terrence Burke, another war veteran who had served with the Irish Guards in the Great War. He was appointed on July 2, 1929, but lasted only two months, being fired on September 4, 1929.[20] Crystal Beach was once again dependent on the OPP until a replacement could be hired.

Immediately after Clunie's dismissal, but prior to the appointment of Terence Burke, another multiple-target OPP raid was conducted on June 22, 1929 involving twenty-three places in Bridgeburg, Erie Beach, and Crystal Beach. It could very well be that the OPP, for operational security reasons, wanted to conduct such a raid without local law enforcement being involved. In the Crystal Beach part of this large operation, charges were laid against Michael Sheehan and Fred George for having liquor in their establishments which was not listed on their permits.[21]

Amidst all of the personnel turnover within the local police department, the Premiere of Ontario, Howard Ferguson ordered an inquiry into the allegations of drunken revelries in the Crystal Beach area.[22]

The next chief to follow Clunie and then Burke would be Frank Reavley. Reavley is yet another chief constable of Crystal Beach to have once been associated with, in one way or another, police scandal and dubious activities.

Originally from Ridgeway, Reavley was appointed as the chief constable of the Village of Port Colborne in 1913.[23] Port Colborne is ten miles west of Crystal Beach on the north shore of Lake Erie. At the time of his appointment, he was the only officer on the force. Eventually, two constables were hired to work under his command. In 1916, three years into Reavley's appointment, the Ontario Temperance Act came into effect. The O.T.A. (commonly referred to as the Act), led to bootlegging and liquor smuggling becoming a very profitable business for many who chose to take advantage of the demand for liquor on both sides of the border. Reavley held the position as chief in Port Colborne until 1925.

In 1919, manufacture for export was made legal in Ontario. Port Colborne is a major port in the Great Lakes system, with access to shipping, railways, and most importantly, the unguarded American shoreline just across the lake. In 1920, U.S. Prohibition came into effect, creating a huge market in the U.S. for legally exported (from Canada), but *illegally* imported (to the U.S) liquor from Canada. A new business opportunity was born, and millions were made.

In April of 1925, Reavley and his entire Port Colborne police force of two constables were all abruptly dismissed by the town council, with no reason being given to the media. The newly-elected council had just recently given Reavley and his men a substantial pay raise to encourage "better efficiency," but after a thorough three-month follow-up study, decided instead to dismiss the entire police force.

The findings of the study were kept in-council and never disclosed to the media or public. Reavley was replaced by George Crowe, a former Detective Sergeant with the Toronto Police. Crowe re-instated one of Reavley's fired constables, James Stevenson, but Constable

Frederick Davis joined Reavley on the unemployment line.[24] Stevenson would eventually serve as Port Colborne's Chief of Police in the 1940s and 50s.

Immediately after his firing, Reavley took a position in Port Colborne in the east-end railway yards as a "liquor watchman" for a group of liquor exporters, who would buy railcars filled with liquor directly from Canadian distilleries for legal export to the United States. His job was to safeguard the locked and sealed boxcars.[25] The mysterious liquor exporting group was unofficially referred to as the "Port Colborne Liquor Syndicate." During this same time period, Al Capone had just taken over the biggest crime outfit in Chicago from Johnny Torrio, and it is widely known that Canada was Capone's largest supplier of illicit liquor.

The boxcars came from Montreal and Manitoba, each one loaded with $25,000 worth of the finest whiskey and rum made in Canada. It would fetch $75,000 on the other side of the lake, a 200 percent profit. At the time, the Ontario Temperance Act prohibited production for the sale of alcohol, but production for export was perfectly legal.

A *Buffalo Courier Express* reporter was given exclusive and confidential access to the syndicate's operations in 1926. The reporter was very guarded as to the ownership of the organization. In one three-week period, the Port Colborne syndicate legally exported from Canada $250,000 worth of Canadian spirits, which then sold for $750,000 at various destinations in the United States. There, it would be further cut with cheaper inferior whiskey, further increasing profits for the end user, too.

Half a million dollars profit on ten car loads. This more than made up for the cost of the booze, its transport by rail, and the excise tax that would be paid on it. Strangely, very little of the product from Port Colborne ever actually went to Buffalo, as much higher prices would be paid for it by customers in the larger eastern seaboard cities.

Since exportation was legal in Canada, the exporters meticulously stuck to the Customs laws and regulations. The Canadian customs officer's only duty and concerns were that the liquor be loaded directly from the boxcars onto the boats, and that the boats immediately depart the port with the product. Many export manifests listed Cuba as the destination country for export, and went unquestioned by customs. As long as the export manifest was signed off by a customs officer, no laws were broken, and the government was happy. The distillers were making money, the exporters were making money, and so was the federal government. Brian Johnson wrote in *Maclean's Magazine*, "The amount of alcohol subject to excise tax—most of which went south one way or another—went from 36,000 litres in 1920 to 5,000,000 only ten years later, and the excise tax on it rose to a fifth of federal revenue, twice as much as income tax."[26]

The cutters that the runners used were very fast and covered in armour plates, but that was for protection against the U.S. authorities once the international boundary was crossed in the middle of the lake. Once in U.S. waters, the Canadian "exporters" then became "smugglers" under American law. The runners would have drivers with very fast cars planted at various obscure locations along the U.S. shore, far from downtown Buffalo, and just take their chances with the U.S. Coast Guard.

At the railway side yards, loads were heavily guarded by private security, Frank Reavley's new job being an example of that function. Loads were counted and checked as they left the boxcars, and then re-counted and re-checked after they were shuttled by trucks to the canal-side. The cargo was immediately loaded onto the boats for export, all done in broad daylight in front of the customs agent, and there was no secrecy about it.[27]

The historical notion that gangsters were clandestinely sneaking around, being pursued by the police in Port Colborne, smuggling liquor in the dead of night is a result of romantic historic embellishment. It was not Chicago. Smuggling goods *into* Canada at Port Colborne, however, was a whole different story and activity, involving different sets of laws, enforcement regulations, and legal risks.

During the days of the Ontario Temperance Act, exporting liquor, as opposed to producing, distributing, and selling, turned out to be the most lucrative option in the Ontario booze business. It was also the safest bet against prosecution. In Canada, that is. Much to the

U.S. authorities' consternation, Port Colborne had amassed the largest rum-running fleet in Lake Erie history. But they were breaking no Canadian laws.[28]

It is very interesting that during this same time, a controversial MPP for Toronto South-East and onetime Federal Member of Parliament, Colonel John Allister Currie, had purchased thirteen acres of land at Killaly Street, right on the east side of the Welland Canal.

In 1925, he built the Highland Scotch Distilleries in Port Colborne, owned by the Dominion Industrial Alcohol Company.[29] Currie, described as a parliamentary "insider," was the leader of the wet side in the ongoing temperance debates.

In 1928, Currie's Conservative Party passed legislation requiring distillers to load their product onto boats for export within twenty-four hours of leaving the distillery, and banning the storage of liquor in rail cars awaiting export.[30] This would essentially put an end to the Port Colborne syndicate's operations in the railway sidings. It would also all but eliminate the distillers from Montreal and Winnipeg from exporting to the U.S. from Port Colborne, as the loads would have great difficulty making it to Port Colborne within the required twenty-four hours. There would also be no legal storage facilities for the shipments to await loading on to boats once arriving in Port Colborne.

Conveniently for Currie, his newly-established Highland Scotch Distillery Company would stand to benefit greatly if the new legislation was passed, as he planned to manufacture right there in Port Colborne, next to the canal.

Surely Currie knew of the astronomical sums of money that the legal exporters of liquor were making in Port Colborne. His intention was to distill and blend fine liquors in the Port Colborne facility and then load it directly onto the rum-runners' boats, docked at canal-side, under the watchful eyes of the Canadian customs officers. The rum-runners were the only ones breaking the law, and even then, only once they crossed into U.S. waters.

After the O.T.A was repealed in 1927, the Highland Scotch Distillery was acquired by a group from Montreal, who purchased even more acreage, with plans to expand the facility. They even brought in two master distillers from Scotland to supervise the blending of the whiskey and liqueurs.[31]

The distillery was sold again in 1936 to James A. Forrest and Company, which produced whiskey and gin brands including Forrest's Red Seal Old Highland Whiskey, Goodwill Pure Rye Whiskey, London Mayfair Dry Gin, Highland Scotch Distillers Special Pure Canadian Rye Whiskey, and Babbling Brook Old Bourbon Whiskey.

Since U.S. Prohibition ended in 1933, the once-lucrative illegal rum-running out of Port Colborne would have decreased dramatically by this time. Forrest may have also legally produced alcohol for industrial and medical purposes at the Port Colborne facility, however there are no further local records of the business after 1940.[32]

The true relationship between Frank Reavley and the mysterious exporter's group prior to his dismissal from the police department may never be known. Reavley later earned a reputation as a law-and-order cop in Crystal Beach. Perhaps the Port Colborne exporters felt that without Reavley as chief of police, their cargo was more vulnerable to thefts and hijackings, and that they needed his "protection" in another capacity. It does seem strange that for years the owners of the liquor-filled boxcars were content as far as security went until Reavley was fired, and only then created the watchman position for him immediately after his firing. Perhaps the syndicate was not yet sure about, or comfortable with, Reavley's replacement and the new police force "adapting" to how the system had always worked in the Port Colborne rail yards and ports.

Port Colborne was and still is a very busy port, and it has always had a colourful reputation as a haven for bootleggers and liquor smuggling. The syndicate may have been correct in feeling that their loads were suddenly vulnerable sitting out on the railway sidings, sometimes for months at a time. In his new position as liquor watchman, Reavley almost immediately began an investigation into alleged hijackings and robberies from those very boxcars awaiting export in the east-end railway sidings.

Reavley's investigation involved the theft of nine cases of whiskey which were stolen from a locked box car on December 16, 1925.

CRYSTAL BEACH: OUT OF THE PARK

Reavley's investigation implicated two Port Colborne police constables, one of whom used to work under him.

The police commission and the new chief, George Crowe, assessed Reavley's complaint and quickly determined that there was, essentially, "nothing to see here," and it was swept under the rug. Chief Crowe publicly vindicated his officers in the press only five days after the theft had occurred. Reavley's complaint went nowhere.[33]

In February, 1926, shortly after Frank Reavley's complaint had been summarily dismissed, he received an appointment to a provincial position as "Examiner of Applicants" for chauffer's licences in the Niagara area.[34] How or why Frank Reavley received such a trusted appointment after having been fired as a police chief is anyone's guess. Perhaps he knew things of a politically sensitive or embarrassing nature regarding the liquor activities that had long taken place in the Port Colborne area. The stories he could tell.

This was, after all, the era of notorious Hamilton mobster Rocco Perri's dominance of the liquor smuggling and bootlegging business in the Golden Horseshoe. Perri had hundreds of government officials and civil servants on his unofficial payroll. Politicians, police officers, customs officers, and government employees were on Perri's "cash only" payroll. The shadowy "Port Colborne Liquor Syndicate" may very well have been connected, or at least paying a cut of their huge legal profits, to Rocco Perri. At the time, he was known to be an exporter for the major distilleries like Seagram's and Gooderham & Worts. It is also believed that one of Perri's associates at the time, Hamilton mobster Frank Sylvester, had business interests in Port Colborne.

One thing is certain. There was something shady taking place in the railway yards in Port Colborne in the years leading up to 1925, which resulted in the entire police department being dismissed.

Frank Reavley enjoyed his provincial license examiner appointment until he was appointed to the Crystal Beach Police in August of 1929, replacing Terence Burke, and Burke's predecessor Edward Clunie.[35] The media announcement did not specify whether Reavley's appointment was as a constable or as the chief constable.

GARY POOLER

Photo: courtesy Mark Chernish

The history of Frank Reavley and the activities in Port Colborne add greater context and background to the rest of this chapter and the next. Good, bad, or inconsequential, it is what Reavley brought to the Village of Crystal Beach Police Department.

Curiously, during Reavley's tenure as chief in Port Colborne, another future Crystal Beach police chief—albeit briefly—Michael O'Leary, also held various law enforcement positions throughout the Niagara area. He was the area Ontario Temperance Act Officer with the OPP, and then became a detective with the Michigan Central Railway in Bridgeburg. O'Leary was fired from the Michigan Central after being charged with alien smuggling by U.S. authorities. If something involved liquor, railway cars, and smuggling, these two men more than likely had crossed paths at some point, and knew each other at least professionally during this time. Michael O'Leary and his adventures are featured in the next chapter.

In the 1930s, it appears that the position of Chief Constable in Crystal Beach may have alternated from time to time between Frank Reavley and James Goodall. Reavley was still referred to in the press as police chief at least until 1938, while James Goodall is referred to as Crystal Beach Police Chief in 1932, when the village council authorized a telephone for his residence.[36] The two men could very well have rotated through the position periodically, as one-year contracts appear to have been the norm for the Crystal Beach police chief position.

CRYSTAL BEACH: OUT OF THE PARK

Goodall, a World War One veteran, had held the position in 1933 when he charged an individual with attempting to bribe him.[37] He was still referred to as the Crystal Beach police chief in a 1934 missing persons case, involving three young boys who died after becoming adrift and lost in a row boat off of Point Abino.[38] Goodall was also cited as the chief of Crystal Beach Police in 1934 when he charged an individual with kicking him.[39] Goodall had also at one time been the Chief of Company Police at the International Nickel Company, and was a member of the Fort Erie Branch of the Royal Canadian Legion.

In keeping with the unusual and bizarre stories that seemed to follow other Crystal Beach police chiefs, Goodall met a gruesome and unfortunate demise. After resigning as chief of the Crystal Beach force in 1941, Goodall went to work for the Canadian National Railway as a brakeman.

In 1944, at the age of fifty-one, he was killed when he slipped off of a coupling between two cars on a moving train in the eastern rail yards in Port Colborne, and was subsequently run over and killed after five boxcars passed over him.[40]

In Crystal Beach, Reavley established himself as a no-nonsense, law-and-order cop. On the Fourth of July weekend in 1936 Chief Reavley, under orders from Reeve Carl Teal, ordered all slot machines, estimated at around fifty, removed from both the village and from the midway at the amusement park. He warned that any machines not removed would be seized and destroyed.[41]

In 1938, Reavley was praised by the Canadian Postmaster for his part in solving an international forgery case by arresting the suspect in Crystal Beach after he had travelled the world eluding capture.[42]

Chief Frank Reavley.

Photo: Sidney Morris Jr. collection

Whatever baggage Frank Reavley had brought to Crystal Beach from the Port Colborne scandal, all media reports and interviews with locals who knew him indicate that he discharged his duties in the village faithfully and with integrity. His wife Florence worked at the waffle stand in the amusement park, and they were a well-liked and respected couple in the community.

After Scott, Strauch, Pinkerton, O'Leary, Burke, and Clunie, Frank Reavley was just another in a long line of men who tried to take on the task of policing the carnival that was Crystal Beach.

In 1951, Frank Reavley's funeral was attended by many from the community, and he was given police honours. His procession received salutes from officers on traffic control at each intersection. His pall bearers included Port Colborne Police Chief Fred Davies, Fort Erie Police Chief Andrew Griffin, Former Crystal Beach Chief Floyd Garrard, former Park Police Chief Bill Diamond, Provincial Constable Jack Sharratt of Ridgeway, and Sergeant James Stevenson of Port Colborne. He was obviously well-respected by the community and his peers.

High turnover of leadership and inner turmoil would continue to dog the Crystal Beach Police Department and village council throughout the ensuing decades.

Chief Floyd Garrard, with retired Chief Frank Reavley.

Photo: Sidney Morris Jr. collection

After Goodall and Reavley, Floyd Garrard was appointed Chief Constable of Crystal Beach in February of 1941. Garrard, from St. Catharines, was a former Henley Regatta rowing champion. In November 1943, two years after his appointment in Crystal Beach, Garrard entered the Canadian Army to serve in World War Two. He fully believed that he would be reinstated to his position as chief upon completion of his military service, under the Dominion Veteran's Reinstatement Act.

L. J. Simpson filled in as acting chief until January of 1944, when village council appointed Percy Mark chief of police during Floyd Garrard's absence. Appointed along with Percy Mark was Sergeant

Garnet Wakelin, who would end up resigning from the village force twice, in 1945 and 1946, both times alleging police and village mismanagement and misconduct.

Upon completion of his military service in April, 1944, Floyd Garrard returned to Crystal Beach and was informed by village council that although he could return to the village police, it would have to be as a constable earning the same pay as the new chief Percy Mark, which was $1,900 per year.

Garrard objected strenuously to this arrangement and sought legal counsel. He filed a complaint, and charges against the village were laid by the National Employment Service Department.[43] Two village councillors, Ernest Dixon and William Holmes, eventually resigned in protest for the council's refusal to return Garrard to his previous position as chief of police, showing support for the ousted chief.[44]

The process dragged on for months, during which Floyd Garrard continued to walk a beat, work night shifts, and follow his replacement's orders. The dispute resulted in several hearings in Niagara Falls court before Magistrate John B. Hopkins. The case was expected to set a legal precedent in the Dominion of Canada regarding the hiring of returning veterans, so the lawyers and magistrates took their time dealing with it carefully, which dragged the case out. Garrard was described as a highly efficient officer, and one who would be very difficult to replace.[45]

Magistrate Hopkins eventually ruled in favour of Garrard, fining the village one hundred dollars and refunding Garrard two month's back salary. However, Hopkins' decision was later reversed by Judge Harold Fuller of the Welland County Court, who ruled that the village had met its obligation by hiring Garrard back as a constable and granting him chief's pay.

Judge Fuller revoked both the fine against the village and the back pay.[46] Floyd Garrard chose not to continue with the Crystal Beach Police Department, and resigned from his position. Percy Mark was retained as Chief Constable.[47]

There was a story told by John E.'s grandson George R. Rebstock from when he was a young man in the early 1940s. One day, while doing his milk delivery rounds for one of the local dairies, he stopped to watch as the police chief of Crystal Beach physically dragged a troublemaker out of the village, up Ridgeway Road to the top of the hill at Farr, and then literally kick him out of the village, down the other side of the hill and into Ridgeway. Old school policing at its finest.

This happened long before the village police got their first cruiser, which explains the physical dragging of the offender. Age, and a fuzzy memory of George's story make it difficult to recall whether the chief of police involved in this story was Percy Mark or Floyd Garrard. Considering the approximate year, and the amount of strength and size needed to perform this particular civic duty, it was more than likely Floyd Garrard, who happened to be a mountain of a man.

As stated previously, Percy Mark's appointment took place on January 17, 1944, while Floyd Garrard was away serving in the military. Chief Mark's family owned a store in the village and the people of the community really seemed to like him.

In 1949, Mark was unjustly suspended for five days over an expired fidelity bond that all chief constables were required to have at that time. This was due to the fact that they had to handle money, whether seized as evidence or collected from fines. Constable John Sandel was named temporary acting chief.

The allegedly "expired" bond was discovered by village council during a review that they were conducting regarding the possibility of replacing the village police (Mark and his three constables) with the Ontario Provincial Police.[48] Apparently, the local political wheels were already in motion by certain members of council to find a way to rid the village of local policing, and bring in the OPP as the preferred police service for Crystal Beach. By doing this, village council would avoid having to oversee the police department directly, as forming a police commission at the time was not possible due to the population requirement.

Residents did not react well to Mark's suspension. The Crystal Beach Taxpayers Association, led by American William Taggart, offered to supply any fidelity bond required by Chief Mark. Taggart claimed "Chief Mark is the only good Chief we've had in 35 years."[49]

Taggart was obviously including the period from 1915 (when the OPP began 'summer only' status in the village) up to the year of incorporation in 1921, when the first Chief of Police, Bill Scott, was actually hired. Through it all, Chief Mark claimed that he "always had the interests of the people at heart."[50]

Approximately 150 angry residents stormed the next council meeting at the village fire hall, demanding Chief Mark's reinstatement. It was pointed out at the meeting by Councillor Claude "Bud" Brewster, who presented evidence of such, that the expiry date of the bond had been interpreted incorrectly by the village solicitor. A motion was then made to cancel Chief Mark's suspension, and it was passed. Sincerest apologies were issued to him by both Reeve Norman Smith and Councillor William Holmes.[51]

Percy Mark resumed his position as chief, but resigned the following year on September 5, 1950. Upon his departure, Chief Mark stated that he had had nothing but conflict with all previous village councils, with the exception of the current one. It was quite honourable for him to say that, since they were the same council that had suspended him the year before. Mark also claimed that the village police force was plagued by poor pay and inadequate equipment and resources for the officers.[52]

Crystal Beach P.D. circa 1946.

L to R: Const. Art Thornton, Const. Bill Sloat, Chief Percy Mark, Const. John Sandel, Sgt. Garnet Wakelin. Photo: courtesy Frank Thornton

CRYSTAL BEACH: OUT OF THE PARK

One major incident that Chief Mark had to deal with during his tenure was the rape of a seventeen-year-old girl from Buffalo. On June 26, 1949, the girl had come to Crystal Beach for the day with her brother and sister. At the beach, they met a young man whom she knew previously from Buffalo, and he invited the girl and her sister back to a cottage. While there, the girl was assaulted and raped by six males, all from Buffalo.[53]

Victor Russo, seventeen, of Buffalo was convicted of rape by a jury and sentenced to three years in Kingston Penitentiary. His lawyer, W. K. Brown of Ridgeway, announced his intention to appeal the verdict and sentence.[54] Later that year, in Ontario Supreme Court Appeals division, Russo's conviction was overturned, citing lack of sufficient evidence.[55] One has to wonder whether Chief Percy Mark's statement when he resigned—that the village police were plagued by inadequate resources—had played a role in the "insufficient evidence" ruling. A sexual assault case involving six male offenders and two young female victims, is beyond the ability of a small four-man police department to investigate properly.

Victor Russo was indeed no angel. Three years later he was arrested in Buffalo and charged with possession of heroin, needles, and strainers. Police claimed that he and his partners were attempting to take over the heroin market in Buffalo.[56]

During Chief Mark's tenure there was also a theft of two firearms from the Crystal Beach police office, one of which was subsequently used in a robbery-homicide case in Buffalo, New York.

On October 19, 1946 Richard Boyd*, eighteen, of Crystal Beach, and John Andrews, seventeen, of Fort Erie had crossed the Peace Bridge to Buffalo via bus. Each had a stolen handgun, a .32 calibre semi-automatic and a .38 calibre revolver, one of them from the Crystal Beach Police Department.

They held up 32-year-old Gerald Goldsman's jewellery store on Genesee Street in Buffalo, and then pistol-whipped him. They took $106 in cash and $128 worth of jewellery. The jewellery was pawned

---

* Author's note: The names of those involved in this case have been changed.

for forty dollars. The pair then travelled back to Canada. On Friday, November 1, Boyd and another member of his "gang," John Hawkins, seventeen, of Fort Erie hitch-hiked a ride from Ridgeway to Buffalo with another young man from Ridgeway. The young man from Ridgeway was neither aware of, nor involved in, any of the subsequent events.

Boyd, Hawkins, and Andrews were all students at Fort Erie High School at the time. Shortly before nine p.m., Boyd and Hawkins entered Sorenson's cigar store on Division Street in Buffalo. Boyd shot and killed the 58-year-old store clerk, John Graf, and the pair made off with $125 in cash.

They were arrested shortly after at the Buffalo Greyhound Bus Terminal. Boyd and Hawkins each had a stolen pistol from Canada in their possession. Boyd had $113 in American cash on him when arrested. Boyd admitted to being the ring leader of the gang, and also confessed to several Toronto and Fort Erie area holdups.

Andrews agreed to return to Buffalo and cooperate with the police after being charged with the first robbery from October 19. Andrews and Boyd directed the police to where they would find a cache of stolen weapons, most of them hidden in the girders under the Peace Bridge on the Canadian side, and others along the shore under the bridge hidden amongst the rocks. Most of this arsenal, a total of seven guns, had been stolen from a smash and grab robbery from a window display at Camm's Drug Store in Fort Erie, in addition to the ones stolen from the Crystal Beach police department.

Boyd also told Police that they had hidden other weapons in the sand under the boardwalk in Crystal Beach. Included in the recovered weapons were seven German Lugers, a P-38 pistol, two .32 calibre pistols, one of them fully-automatic, along with numerous magazines and ammunition. Boyd and Hawkins were held in custody pending an appearance before the Grand Jury.[57]

In 1947, Boyd and Hawkins were both found guilty of armed robbery and murder and given life sentences, to be served at Attica Correctional Facility.[58] After numerous failed appeals, Boyd was released in 1967 as part of an arrangement which had him plead guilty to manslaughter for the killing of John Graf, and then receive credit for the twenty years that he had already served.

Chief Mark also had to deal with the death of a village man who was crushed to death by a trailer that he was working on, and also a safe burglary at the Crystal Beach Amusement Company by three summer employees of the park. He worked on the burglary case with William Diamond, referred to as a special policeman with the Crystal Beach Amusement Company.[59]

These types of serious occurrences are normally very difficult to investigate even for a larger, well-equipped police force. Chief Mark and his department, with their limited resources, equipment, and training, would frequently be in way over their heads in such investigations.

Chief Mark also displayed his humanity when he arranged to have his own family take custody of a homeless girl who had been charged with theft. He told the court that the girl had no parents or relatives, no home, and that she believed no one was concerned with her welfare. The girl smiled in court when Chief Mark told the court that he had raised five children, and that he could place her in the home of one of his adult married children. The court placed her under the care of Mark's family, and the charge was dismissed.[60]

After leaving the Crystal Beach Police Department, Chief Percy Mark returned to Lindsay, Ontario, where he had previously been on the police force, to enter into private business.[61]

The next Chief to take on the Crystal Beach job lasted only seven months. Bernard Kitney, a former OPP Constable, started the job in September 1950, succeeding Percy Mark, but abruptly resigned the following year in April of 1951, having never led the force through even one summer of Crystal Beach chaos.[62]

Perhaps he saw the writing on the wall after what Percy Mark had been through, the vigilance group's bootlegging allegations, and the uncomfortable familiarity that his men had with the local population. He may have seen things that he did not approve of. In July of 1951, Kitney would later represent Constable John Sandel at a village council meeting following Sandel's suspension. Bernard Kitney later became Chief Constable in Bowmanville, Ontario.[63]

GARY POOLER

Bernard Kitney, left, and Bowmanville Police Force, circa 1960.

Photo: Courtesy Myno Van Dyke

In May of 1951, Gilbert Robertson, another former OPP constable, became Crystal Beach's third police chief in ten months. Most of Robertson's policing experience with the OPP had been as a motorcycle patrolman, assigned to Fort Erie, Aurora, Lambeth, and Scarborough. He had twice been dismissed from the OPP, once in 1934, but was re-hired in 1935. He was fired again in 1948. Three years later, he became chief of police in Crystal Beach.

When Robertson took the position in May of 1951, it was at the height of the bootlegging accusations being made by the vigilance committee, and it was also right at the start of the summer season. Robertson inherited a simmering can of worms. In addition to experiencing his first Memorial Day opening in Crystal Beach, shortly thereafter a horrific murder would take place only a month after he took the position. Gilbert Robertson would not be the first police chief to experience conflict with village council, but he would certainly be the last.

Robertson, like most of his predecessors, was unlikely prepared for the fact that policing in Crystal Beach was nothing like any of them had ever experienced before. Imagine being a former motorcycle patrolman and becoming the chief of police in a small village of one thousand people, only to have that small quiet village, on any given weekend, turn into a wild, overpopulated carnival of seventy thousand people from May until Labour Day, every summer.

Allegations of police laxity were levelled by both the vigilance committee members and the village reeve, Claude Brewster. Brewster claimed that on one busy weekend he could not find any of the constables on duty, and had to call Constable Clarence Ott in on overtime. Chief Robertson, who had only just started the job, countered that he had to deal with a crowd of over seventy thousand people in the village on a recent weekend. He claimed that he had gone fifteen days without sleep, and that he and his men did not even have a proper police station. This was definitely not motorcycle patrol.

The vigilance committee petitioned the Ontario Attorney General to send in the OPP to clean up the mess. One committee member even alleged that some council members and police officers in the village had been receiving payoffs in order to stifle criminal prosecutions.[64]

Some village council members felt that the complaints were simply political vindictiveness following the previous election in 1950. Claude Brewster had narrowly defeated local businessman William Holmes, a former village councillor and owner of the Ontario Hotel, in a bitter three-way race for Reeve. Others claimed that the rowdyism and disturbances were no more than what would normally be expected at any other summer resort town.[65]

One month into Chief Robertson's tenure, in June of 1951, things took a very serious turn when an alleged local bootlegger was murdered. Some members of the village council and the vigilance group, pegged her involvement in the illicit business as the reason behind the killing. It turned out to be the result of a lover's dispute, but the vigilance group used the hysteria of the murder to bolster their claims that a crime wave was running rampant in the village.[66]

Mrs. Leone (Peterson) Bassett, a forty-nine-year-old divorcee from Buffalo, lived at 34 Cambridge Road East with her common-law husband, Edward Anthony Bassett, forty-seven, also formerly of Buffalo. (Please note: this is no longer the same street address where this event occurred). Mrs. Bassett, whose maiden name was Bailey, was also known locally as Leone Peterson, having been divorced for several years from a Buffalo man named Peterson.

She ran the place on Cambridge as a boarding house which she named the "Chateau Flamingo." It was common knowledge throughout the village that she was engaged in bootlegging.[67]

Her common-law husband, Edward Bassett, was an electrician at the American Brass Company in Buffalo. He had been separated, but not divorced from, Jessie Bassett of Williamsville, New York for eighteen years. Edward and Leone had been involved with each other for the past eleven years, and had shared the Cambridge Road address in a common-law relationship since 1948.

On June 15, 1951, Leone Bassett had met Steve Conscul, a Hungarian refugee living in Crystal Beach, in front of one of the Crystal Beach hotels and had invited him back to the Flamingo for a drink. It was most likely the Imperial Hotel on Cambridge where they met, as it was just doors away from the Flamingo. One can draw their own conclusions about what the two were planning to do at 34 Cambridge, but it turned out to involve booze, sex, and murder.

Just after midnight in the village, in the wee hours of June 16, 1951, Mrs. Bassett, Steve Conscul and two other women, Margaret Jansen and Celia Gamble, were drinking whiskey at the Chateau Flamingo.

Conscul testified that he next remembered that in the early morning of Saturday, June 16, he was awakened by a punch to the face by Edward Bassett. Bassett had come home at eight a.m. after working all night in Buffalo and found Conscul and Mrs. Bassett in bed, both asleep.

Conscul testified that he got up and asked Ed Bassett to hand him his pants, and then quickly vacated the premises. Conscul witnessed Edward Bassett slap Mrs. Bassett as he made his exit.[68]

In court, Police Chief Gilbert Robertson testified that later that same day, while sitting in his police vehicle, he had been approached by Mrs. Bassett who seemed agitated. She asked Robertson if he would accompany her home, as she and Ed had been fighting all day after Ed found her in bed with another man. Robertson further testified that Mrs.

Bassett had told him "I am very ill-tempered, and I might murder him if I go alone."

Robertson accompanied Mrs. Bassett home, and the last time he saw her alive, she was sitting outside on the front steps, locked out of the house.[69] Sadly, the Bassett residence was literally less than two hundred metres around the corner from the village police office.

Not to judge Chief Robertson through the filter of time, but his actions that day are completely at odds with current-day policing policies and procedures in regards to domestic cases. He had received information from one of the parties that a domestic situation was in progress. Mrs. Bassett was agitated, and she also told the Chief that she "might murder" Ed if she were to go home alone. Ed had already slapped her. Robertson should have at least gotten out of his car and spoken with both parties separately to assess the potential risk of violence.

With it being a domestic situation, and after actually hearing the word "murder" uttered from one of the involved parties, Robertson should have at least inquired about any possible weapons in the residence and secured them. Yet he left her sitting there, locked out on the front steps of the residence, just around the corner from the police office, without resolving the conflict or arranging temporary living arrangements for the two parties to be safely separated. This decision by Chief Robertson and its fatal consequences no doubt formed a large part of Reeve Brewster's accusations of police laxity in the aftermath.

Edward Basset testified that he had told Leone to leave and had locked her out of the house all day. She left and came back several times, the last time throwing several objects through the glass of the front door, and gaining access. Angry, she demanded that Edward sign over half of the property to her.

During the argument, she saw that Edward had cut up all of her dresses, and flew into a rage, throwing three beer bottles at him, striking him in the head and arms. Edward then retrieved a shotgun from the closet, with the intention (according to him) of "scaring her."

Leone turned and ran towards the front door, Edward following her with the loaded shotgun. After exiting the front door, she made a quick right turn on the veranda towards the stairs leading down to the ground, which were on the left side in the photo below. As she approached the stairs, Ed shot her in the back of the head from close range, blowing the back of her head almost completely off. Her body continued down the stairs from the impact of the round, and landed face-down on the ground near the bottom of the stairs. She was dead before she hit the ground. Edward claimed it was accidental.[70]

Chateau Flamingo, scene of the Bassett murder.

Photo: Courtesy Shawn Moore

Immediately after, a young boy approached village constable Wilfred Teal and informed him that a woman had "fainted" over on Cambridge.

Teal arrived at the cottage shortly after seven p.m. to find Mrs. Bassett's body on the ground next to the front porch steps, obviously dead from a shotgun blast to the head. Constable Teal retrieved a hammock from the front porch and covered the victim's body with it.

Chief Robertson testified that he and Constable John Sandel arrived at the scene and along with Constable Teal, entered the residence. While the police were in an upstairs bedroom, a shot rang out from downstairs. Running downstairs to investigate the shot, they found the kitchen door locked. They left the residence, then re-entered with provincial police.

CRYSTAL BEACH: OUT OF THE PARK

While trying to force open a second downstairs bedroom door, another shot rang out from inside the locked room. The officers, after initially taking cover, forced the second bedroom door open, and inside they found Edward Bassett, severely wounded in the head, neck, and left arm area from gunshot wounds.[71] Edward Bassett was transported to Douglas Memorial Hospital in serious condition, where he was charged with first degree murder. Bassett uttered to the police, "As God is my judge, I loved her. I didn't mean to shoot."[72]

Due to the lack of resources and training of the village police department, and the fact that Chief Robertson was a primary witness in the case, Detective Inspector Thomas R. Wright of the Ontario Provincial Police Criminal Investigation Branch was called in to re-construct the scene and oversee the investigation.[73]

The "vigilance" group and the anti-bootlegging politicians both immediately drew a connection between the alleged bootlegging activities of Mrs. Bassett and her murder.[74] The connection appears to have been somewhat justified. She was, after all, serving whiskey and beer to people the night before she was murdered, and the activities at the Chateau Flamingo were known to many in the village, especially Constable Sandel, who had unsuccessfully tried to put a stop to it.

Unbelievably, in September, 1950, Edward Bassett was acquitted of the charges by a jury after only twenty minutes of deliberation. Justice C. Dalton Wells thanked the jury, but also suggested that they had just increased the risks of married life with their verdict.[75]

The tragedy of the Bassett incident did not end with Edward's acquittal, however. Two years later, on October 24, 1953, Edward Anthony Bassett, went to Mount Calvary Cemetery in Cheektowaga, N.Y., once again planning to blow his brains out with a shotgun. This time, however, he succeeded. A cemetery worker discovered Ed's lifeless body. A note found in his car read simply "Call Mrs. Wilma Bassett."

Edward's final misfortune was, again, the result of marital discord. After his acquittal for the murder of Leone Peterson in 1951, Ed Bassett had moved back to Buffalo and married a woman named Wilma. However, he failed to tell his new bride Wilma that he was still legally married to his first wife from years earlier, Jessie Bassett of Williamsville,

N.Y., and that he also had two children with her. When Wilma found this out, she left Ed after only two weeks of marriage and filed for an annulment. These events precipitated a despondent Edward Anthony Bassett going to the cemetery and committing suicide.[76]

Steve Conscul, the unfortunate Hungarian newcomer to Canada, carried the incident with him for the rest of his life. According to local folklore, he drowned his demons with whiskey, to the point that he became known locally to the few who knew him as "Whiskey Steve."

The aftermath of the gruesome murder of Leone Peterson Bassett did bring everyone in the village's attention to the fact that for whatever reason, law and order in Crystal Beach was in very bad need of improvement. It also got the attention of the provincial government. The village always had a very high turnover rate of both constables and chiefs since its inception. From the time of village incorporation until the OPP takeover in 1951, Crystal Beach had thirteen different police chiefs in thirty years, culminating with the last three within a period of only ten months.[77]

Conflict and scandal continued immediately after the Bassett murder. Two weeks later, on the busy Fourth of July weekend, Chief Robertson suspended Constable John Sandel, a vocal opponent of both the bootleggers, and the lenience shown towards them. Robertson claimed the suspension had been for refusing an order. Apparently, the "order" was for Sandel to stand down on his enforcement efforts against local bootleggers. There are other opinions as to why Sandel had been suspended, but the official one given by Robertson was for refusing an order. Reeve Claude Brewster, in turn, immediately fired Chief Robertson for "laxity" in his duties.

The Chief of the Volunteer Fire Department, George Pietz was then fired for conduct unbecoming after Brewster alleged that Pietz, angered at Sandel's suspension, had threatened Chief Robertson's wife and daughter. Pietz denied the allegations.

This resulted in the entire Volunteer Fire Department resigning in support of their chief, and demanding his immediate reinstatement. The firemen outright defied Brewster, and voted Pietz back in as chief at their very next meeting. This both complicated matters and angered Brewster even further. However, he would not budge, and made arrangements with the Ridgeway Fire Department to provide fire services to Crystal Beach, and for the Bertie Township OPP to provide policing services to the village. Sandel was reinstated pending a hearing and Pietz was eventually reinstated as fire chief.[78] Robertson would not be so fortunate. His services were terminated, and his firing from July 3, 1951 was upheld.[79] It truly was a mess, and the community was in crisis.

In the 1950 photo below, Constable John Sandel is shown "arresting" Fifi the Clown. The photo is an appropriate image for the time, given what the village and the police department were going through. The clown in the photo, Fifi, was in reality Richard O'Mahony, a former orphan child who came to Canada as one of the British Home Children. He completed his indentured service in 1926 at the age of twenty-one, and became a clown. His life could be a movie.

Fifi the Clown performed across the country with Bernardi's Circus, the Garden Brothers Circus, and was a regular at the Canadian National Exhibition from the 1940s until the 1980s. He became quite famous in Canada, and was engaged more than once by the Crystal Beach Amusement Park. It is not known what Fifi did in Crystal Beach which resulted in him being arrested by Constable Sandel. Hopefully, it did not involve anything Stephen King-ish.

Photo: Courtesy Gary Sandel

With no police chief in the village, Ontario Provincial Police Corporal Gerald Lynch was brought in from Welland to lead two OPP constables, C. J. Kruger from Cayuga, and Jack Audsley from Niagara Falls. Lynch was also placed in charge of the four remaining village constables.[80] This arrangement would remain in place until the policing situation in Crystal Beach could be straightened out.

Village council had long wanted to distance themselves from directly overseeing the police department. There were attempts at forming a Police Commission, but the village learned that this could not be done within a community of less than five thousand year-round residents. If council did not want to oversee the police, the only alternative was to employ the OPP.

In addition to a formal request for help to Ontario Attorney General Dana Porter, a survey was also conducted by Provincial Police Inspector Christopher Airey. The purpose was to determine the needs and problems of policing in Crystal Beach, and how many officers would be required throughout the different seasons.[81]

Less than a month after the Bassett murder, the OPP swooped in and raided a bootlegger's cottage at 35 Cambridge Road East, right across the street from the "Chateau Flamingo"—the scene of the Bassett murder. This place was known as "Tony's Inn," in line with the Crystal Beach tradition of cottage-naming, even if you were running a bootlegging operation. A third residence was raided at 9 Cambridge Road East. Three men were charged with illegal sale of liquor, and fifteen people, nine of them Americans, were charged with being "found-ins."

The raids were conducted at two a.m. and were done without the prior knowledge or involvement of any members of the village police force. None of the OPP officers involved in the raid were from the area.[82] Twelve days later, Police Magistrate John Hopkins threw the book at the accused bootleggers, setting a new record for liquor fines in finding Anthony Piccolo of Buffalo and Harry Clark of Hamilton both guilty of bootlegging. They were fined $500 each, which is the equivalent to approximately $5,000 in today's funds.[83]

This was an obvious statement being made by the judicial system in general, and the Ontario Provincial Police in particular, that the fun and games in respect to bootlegging in Crystal Beach were over. The grudging yet inevitable takeover of policing in Crystal Beach by the OPP was under way.

The village reeve, Claude Brewster declared that he would not seek re-election if the village continued with a local police force. He believed that the OPP was the only sensible solution, as it was just too difficult to police a small village with local people also being the local constabulary. This sense of familiarity with the village population and the seasonal summer residents was seen by some as the main barrier to effective law enforcement.

Crystal Beach is only one-square mile in area. In those days, there were perhaps one thousand year-round residents. In the summer, there were upwards of twenty-five thousand summer residents, in addition to another twenty thousand or so more park visitors from May until Labour Day. That is a very small area to police that many people, and it would be very difficult for a local officer to professionally distance himself in an occurrence involving friends or family, which inevitably happened on almost every call in such a small area of responsibility. According to the vigilance group, the familiarity between the village police and the bootleggers had existed for years.

Photo: Author

On July 17, 1951, village council voted to overhaul the village's policing situation. Requests had already been made to both the Ontario Provincial Police Commissioner and the Ontario Attorney

General for help. After inquiries and investigations, and with the Bassett murder and bootlegging allegations no doubt factoring in, the Village of Crystal Beach entered into a municipal policing contract with the Ontario Provincial Police. The OPP were given responsibility for the year-round policing duties within the village, and assumed duty on October 3, 1951.[84]

For American readers and baseball fans, this is the same day that Bobby Thompson hit the "Shot Heard 'Round the World" at the Polo Grounds in New York, winning the National League pennant for the Giants. It was also the first nationally-televised Major League Baseball game.

The entire village police force was subsequently disbanded. In Crystal Beach, it could be referred to as the "Shot Heard 'Round the Village," as the residents were stunned by the announcement.

Corporal Lynch was put in charge of Provincial Constables Claude Kruger and Gord Collins. The Crystal Beach OPP detachment would have three officers from October to May, then increase to four in June, then increase to seven officers for July to September. Lynch would be succeeded shortly thereafter by Corporal Ed Legate.

Throughout the remainder of the 50s and into the 60s, OPP officers maintained the peace and gained the respect of the residents, both year-round and seasonally. The OPP officers were able to maintain their professional distance, yet engaged with the community in many events such as the Alpsfest, the Bavarian bed races and the annual End-of-Summer parade. They were respected, and maybe even a little bit feared. As a kid, when the OPP told you to go home, you went home. Several raised families in the area, and joined the Kinsmen and other service clubs.

There were several year-round officers, who were bolstered by additional manpower deployed to the Beach just for the summer months. New summer officers were cycled in periodically over the years, preventing the over-familiarity that had plagued the village force in previous decades. There were no more police or bootlegging scandals, but it has never been totally eradicated in the village. In the 1940s the vigilance committee alleged that there were sixty or more bootleggers within the village. Today, they can be counted on one hand, although some year-round residents would claim otherwise.

In the following decades there were a few public disorder incidents, most notably a fight between two fraternities which turned into a mini riot on Derby Road. Theta Kappa Phi was a local Crystal Beach fraternity, nothing like the preppy image of a fraternity as seen on television. Known as "Kappa," the Crystal Beach frat was much closer to a street gang than a fraternity, and they would fight anyone who was looking for one. Crystal Beach was Kappa's turf, and every summer a new group from the outside would try to assert themselves in the Beach.

Kappa Beta, a frat from Buffalo, was basically the same thing as Kappa, a gang of young tough guys who would fight anyone who crossed them. A scuffle broke out between the two groups in the summer of 1969, when KB was staying at a place on Derby Road. There was sporadic fighting, along with beer bottles being flung off of the upper veranda of the KB cottage.

The situation escalated to the point where the village reeve at the time, Albert Opatovsky, attended the scene with the Riot Act in hand, intending to invoke it upon the combatants to cease and desist. It didn't get to that point, as fire hoses were used to disperse the crowd.

The OPP called in reinforcements, including the Riot Squad, and dozens were arrested, but this incident did not reach the scale of the infamous 1956 *Canadiana* gang fight. Local legend has it that the ongoing dispute between Kappa and Kappa Beta was eventually settled with an *unofficially* police-sanctioned fight between the presidents of each group over at the Crystal Beach Stadium. The home team won convincingly. Again, *as legend has it*.

In July of 1977, the Satan's Choice Motorcycle Club rented a place in Crystal Beach for a week-long patch-over ceremony/party. The Choice hosted club members from across Ontario to take part in burning their colours and "patching over" to the Outlaws Motorcycle Club. Although visually terrifying to many residents, this gathering caused no real public disturbances on the scale of the "riots." There were a lot of noise complaints from the Harleys and the parties, and the police did gather a lot of important intelligence on the attendees and their vehicles.

Nine chapters of the Satan's Choice changed allegiances to the Outlaws that weekend. After the ceremony, the bikers left the village the same way they arrived, with hundreds of rumbling Harleys roaring out of the village, now wearing their new Outlaws colours.

Even with the Outlaws gone and the bootlegging stopped, it didn't mean the end of periodic incidents of murder or mayhem after the village dissolved in 1970-71.

In the late 70s, a jealous admirer nicknamed Watoos walked up to a young woman that he had perceived as having jilted him, and shot her point-blank in the head at the Hébert's Hotel. The victim survived the shooting, but Watoos, distraught over thinking that he had killed her, went into a semi-abandoned barber shop next door to the Hébert's Hotel and shot himself in the head, taking his own life. He was found the next day.

On May 4 1977, an eccentric and sodden gentleman named Harry Elliott was killed by a shotgun blast during an argument with an alleged bootlegger at 14 Shannon Road.[85]

In addition to the attempted murder at the Hébert's, and the Harry Elliott shooting, there were four other more recent homicides within the Village of Crystal Beach boundaries. One occurred in the 1970s, and three happened in the early 2000s.

One of these cases was featured in a well-known U.S. publication's section featuring true but bizarre crimes. The story goes that a Crystal Beach couple was involved in a domestic dispute while under the influence of alcohol. The man happened to be missing an arm and wore a prosthetic one in its place. The argument escalated into a physical fight, during which the woman yanked off the man's fake arm and proceeded to beat him to death with it.[86]

In August 2001, an elderly male, John Maloney, was killed at his residence at 321 Ridgeway Road, less than two hundred metres around the corner from where Harry Elliott had been killed on Shannon Road. Through a plea agreement, a 27-year-old woman pleaded guilty to the lesser charge of manslaughter in Maloney's death.[87]

CRYSTAL BEACH: OUT OF THE PARK

In the mid-2000s, a male party was shot and killed at a residence on Cherrywood Avenue in Crystal Beach.

In 2005, David Hugh McIntee shot Raam Shankar Pershadsingh five times at a residence on Lincoln Road East, killing him. Pershadsingh's body was discovered weeks later by a municipal employee doing a utility check. McIntee entered a guilty plea to second-degree murder, and received a life sentence.[88]

Bear in mind the low population and small area of the village itself if statistically analyzing these events. All of them involved Canadian year-round residents, rather than summer residents or visitors. The incidents described here do not include events from the surrounding areas of Ridgeway, Bay Beach, or Point Abino, etc. In 1921 the village population was 298. In 1961, it increased to just under two thousand with twenty-five thousand summer residents.[89] Today, the same area has a population of approximately eight thousand year-round residents.[90]

Since Crystal Beach's first *recorded* homicide, the 1951 Bassett murder, a total of seven attempted or actual homicides have occurred within the 340-acre area of the Village of Crystal Beach in the past seventy years. That is one murder every ten years within the boundary of Schooley Road, Erie Road, Ridgeway Road, and Farr Avenue, later including the area south of Rebstock from Ridgeway Road, east to South Ridge Road. Actually, all of these violent acts took place within the village inside an even *smaller* area no larger than two football fields, and all east of Derby Road. Whether these are positive, negative, or even insignificant statistics in regards to murder rate per geographic area, is best left to the criminologists, sociologists, and crime statisticians. It could also mean that it's healthier to live west of Derby Road.

In general, the Wild West days of the mid-1900s in Crystal Beach declined along with the amusement park, which closed permanently in 1989. Today, a reasonable level of law and order had been established in Crystal Beach.

After the amalgamation of all communities into the Regional Municipality of Niagara in 1970, the OPP continued on in the village, even after the formation of the Niagara Regional Police Service. This is likely due to the nature of the summer population, and the historical need for extra law enforcement in the village during the summer. In 1977, the OPP detachment in Crystal Beach was permanently closed, and all responsibility for policing in the former Village of Crystal Beach was assumed by the Niagara Regional Police Service.

Upon completion of a four p.m. to midnight shift in the spring of 1977, Provincial Constable Jerry Deheus became the final OPP Constable to serve in Crystal Beach, Ontario, completing the duties that started with Provincial Constable Jackson back in 1915. Deheus turned out the lights, locked the detachment door, and handed the keys over to Sgt. Doug Conhiser of the recently-formed Niagara Regional Police. It was the end of an era.

Provincial Constable J. Deheus, the last OPP Constable to serve in Crystal Beach.

Photo: Courtesy Jerry Deheus

CHAPTER SIX:
MICHAEL JOHN O'LEARY, V.C.

Little is known about the individual Chief Constables of the Crystal Beach Police Department prior to their showing up in the village to take on the job. Some had prior policing experience in other police services in one form or another. Some were military veterans.

One Crystal Beach police chief, however, stands out from the rest as far as life exploits go. He once won a two-hour gun battle against two criminals as a Mountie in Saskatchewan, and he killed eight enemy soldiers in one courageous solo attack during World War One. He gained international fame as a war hero and Victoria Cross recipient, and also subsequent notoriety for his nefarious activities in Canada. This larger-than-life character who had achieved world fame, somehow ended up as the police chief in the tiny village of Crystal Beach, Ontario. His story more than deserves its own chapter. He met with King George V, dined with the Prince of Wales, and was written about by Rudyard Kipling and George Bernard Shaw. He was a recipient of the Victoria Cross, the United Kingdom's highest award for bravery in combat. His name was Michael John O'Leary, of Cork County, Ireland.

As much of a black mark on Crystal Beach law and order that the events of the late 40s and early 50s may have been, there had already been an equally scandalous, yet lesser-known event involving the Village of Crystal Beach Police Department and its chief at the time, Michael O'Leary. It happened in 1925, some twenty-five years before the bootlegging and murder scandal and subsequent disbanding of the village police department.

Chief of Police Michael John O'Leary.

Photo: www.memorialstovalour.co.uk

In 1925, the chief of police in Crystal Beach was a man named George Pinkerton, who had been appointed in 1923. His last name was certainly famous in the field of law enforcement. Of course, it would be nearly impossible to establish if he was any relation to Allan Pinkerton, of the famous Pinkerton Detective Agency, and the unofficial "founder" of the U.S. Secret Service. Curiously, the amusement park later actually employed Pinkerton agents in the 1940s and 50s.

In June of 1925, at a Crystal Beach village council meeting, George Pinkerton was abruptly informed by Reeve Patrick Ryan that his services as police chief were no longer required. Then—*at the very same meeting*—village council announced that Michael John O'Leary, a World War One hero and Victoria Cross recipient, would replace Pinkerton as Crystal Beach's chief of police, effective July 1, 1925.

One prominent resident of Crystal Beach complained at the meeting that the bootlegging elements had been getting away with far too much, to which O'Leary replied, "I believe I know the duties of this office and shall discharge them fully and fearlessly."[1] The termination of Pinkerton, the citizen's comment, and O'Leary's statement all indicate that bootlegging had been a problem in Crystal Beach, and that O'Leary was more likely brought in to clean it up.

O'Leary's appointment officially took effect on July 1, 1925, and it was announced with much fanfare in several major newspapers on both sides of the border, all of them celebrating the war hero's deeds of bravery in World War One. Unknown at that time however, events of the spring and summer of 1925 would dictate George Pinkerton's return to his old position as police chief within only two months of being ousted.

Michael John O'Leary was born September 29, 1890, in Macroom, Cork County, Ireland. His grave marker indicates a birth date of January 1, 1890. Some researchers establish his year of birth as 1888.

O'Leary joined the British Navy at age sixteen and was assigned to a shore installation at Devonport as a Stoker on the *H.M.S. Vivid*. He left shortly after due to rheumatism in his knees, and returned home. A few months later in 1910, after tiring of the boredom and drudgery of working on the family farm, he left home once again and joined the Irish Guards Regiment of the British Army.

After three years in the Irish Guards, discontent struck him once again and he left Britain for Canada and joined the Royal Northwest Mounted Police, forerunners of the Royal Canadian Mounted Police. During his short time (one year) with the Mounties, O'Leary received a commendation for his bravery in capturing two criminals following a two-hour gun battle in Saskatchewan. He was awarded a gold ring from the RCMP for his actions under fire, which he wore for the rest of his life.[2] Today, he is honoured by the government of Saskatchewan with a memorial plaque for V.C. recipients at the RCMP Training Depot in Regina.

In August 1914, upon the outbreak of World War One, O'Leary received permission from the RNWMP to return to England to re-join the British Army. By November of that year, he had rejoined his Irish Guards unit in France, and immediately received several commendations for bravery, along with a field promotion to Lance Corporal. He obviously craved being in the thick of the action, wherever it was.

On February 1, 1915 at Cuinchy, France, O'Leary would make his mark on history.

The Irish Guards were tasked with supporting the Coldstream Guards in taking a German position along the La Bassee Canal, at a key intersection with a railway line.[3]

With his unit pinned down and having taken heavy casualties, and with most of the British officers either killed or wounded, O'Leary took it upon himself to charge forward, past his entire unit, and run directly into heavy machine gun fire towards a German gun position on the top of a railway embankment.[4] Having previously experienced and won a two-hour gun battle back in Canada during his tenure with the Mounties, was O'Leary emboldened into believing that he could also win this fight? What went through his mind just prior to deciding to stand up and charge towards an actively firing machine gun? Perhaps he decided that he and his unit were all going to die anyway, so why not go down fighting. Or, maybe the stubborn Irishman within him actually believed that he could get to the machine gun nest and neutralize it himself. The word amongst the men in his unit was that O'Leary had simply taken an extreme personal dislike towards one particular member of the German machine gun crew firing at them, and simply wanted to kill him. Only Michael John O'Leary knows the answers to these questions.

One also has to wonder about the thoughts of the young German machine gun crew, and what they were thinking as this apparent madman got closer and closer to their position.

WW1 German machine gun crew.

Photo: period5team1.weebly.com

CRYSTAL BEACH: OUT OF THE PARK

Reaching the railway embankment and the machine gun nest, O'Leary killed all five Germans of the gun crew with five shots, neutralizing the position.[5] This is an incredible physical feat, considering that O'Leary was under heavy fire, adrenaline coursing through his veins, and that he had just sprinted one hundred metres or more wearing heavy equipment, including a coat, boots, helmet, pack, and carrying a rifle.

Compare this to the biathlon competition (cross-country skiing and shooting) in the Winter Olympic Games. Those athletes train for years to learn how to lower their heart and respiration rates after extreme exertion, to be able to steady their rifle and accurately shoot at a target which is static and not shooting back at them. For O'Leary to be able to raise and steady his rifle after his mad dash to the embankment, and then kill all five crew members with only five shots is nothing short of a superhuman effort.

The machine gun positions that O'Leary charged were most likely armed with the tripod-mounted German Maschinengewehr, or MG-08, a water-cooled weapon which was prone to jams, stoppages, and overheating if the coolant ran out. The MG-08 required a crew of five, and was fed ammunition via a cloth or metal belt into the side of the weapon. It had the fire power of sixty to one hundred individual rifles. The MG-08 required enormous amounts of water to keep it from overheating, and crews were not above urinating into the coolant reservoir to keep the weapon functioning. Perhaps prior to making his courageous dash towards the gun position, O'Leary was astute enough under pressure to realize that the German gun was overheating or experiencing a mechanical stoppage, and he made his move during that precise moment.[6]

German Maschinengewehr MG-08.

Photo: en.wikipedia.org

After dispatching the first German gun crew, O'Leary then had the presence of mind to disable the machine gun, rendering it useless. He then spotted, and started taking fire from, a second German machine gun position sixty yards further along the embankment.

Once again, O'Leary, defying all common sense and logic, charged straight towards the second position, again under heavy gun fire. The crew of the second German gun position had obviously just witnessed only seconds before what this man had done to the first crew. And now, this fearless and angry Irishman was charging straight towards them. The young Germans were probably scared to death by this man's obvious courage and sheer savagery.

Upon reaching the second German position, he killed three members of that gun crew and, having run out of ammunition, captured the last two Germans at the point of his bayonet.[7]

After O'Leary's actions, the British were then able to re-capture this strategically vital position at the juncture of the railway and the canal.

Throughout his entire solo attack on these two positions, O'Leary did not suffer so much as a scratch. His fellow soldiers claimed that when he returned to the British line with his two prisoners, he was apparently "as cool as if he had been for a walk in the park."[8]

For his actions that day, O'Leary was given an immediate field promotion to Sergeant and was nominated for and received the Victoria

CRYSTAL BEACH: OUT OF THE PARK

Cross, the highest award for valour in the British military. The wording of his presentation from the London Gazette was:

> No. 3556 Lance-Corporal Michael O'Leary, 1st Battalion, Irish Guards.
>
> For conspicuous bravery at Cuinchy on the 1st February, 1915. When forming one of the storming parties which advanced against the enemy's barricades, he rushed to the front and himself killed five Germans who were holding the first barricade, after which he attacked a second barricade, about 60 yards further on, which he captured, after killing three of the enemy and making prisoners of two more. Lance-Corporal O'Leary thus practically captured the enemy's position by himself and prevented the attacking party from being fired upon.[9]

On June 22, 1915, he was presented with his medal by King George at Buckingham Palace. Parades and receptions were held in his honour, and tributes were written by many prominent people, including George Bernard Shaw and Sir Arthur Conan Doyle.[10] Doyle, known by most as the creator of Sherlock Holmes, wrote of O'Leary "The Irish have always had a reputation of being wonderful fighters, and Lance-Corporal Michael O'Leary is clearly one of them."[11]

Hundreds of thousands of people gathered at Hyde Park in London on July 10, 1915, to celebrate him and to hear him speak. There exists a grainy video file on the internet of O'Leary's 1915 reception at Hyde Park which shows the size of the crowd that came out to honour him.

O'Leary was also further promoted to the rank of Second Lieutenant. As a result of his fame and valour, O'Leary was assigned to a public relations role within the British Army, touring the United Kingdom encouraging other young men, especially in Ireland, to serve. The British Army even created a recruiting poster with O'Leary's image on it, detailing his heroic actions in France.[12]

Image: Library of Congress

In 1921, O'Leary, without his wife Greta and their children, returned to Canada with the intention of re-joining the Royal North West Mounted Police, which had since been re-named the Royal Canadian Mounted Police (RCMP). For reasons unknown, his plan to re-join the Mounties did not materialize, and O'Leary subsequently joined the Ontario Provincial Police as a Temperance Officer out of Dunnville enforcing liquor laws under the Ontario Temperance Act.[13] His area of responsibility would most likely have included the Niagara Peninsula area.

O'Leary resigned from the OPP on June 15, 1923, and took a position as a detective with the Michigan Central Railway based in Bridgeburg, known today as Fort Erie.[14] He was then rejoined by his wife and family in Canada, which would have immediately increased O'Leary's financial burdens.

In 1925, only two years after joining the railway, O'Leary was arrested and charged by the U.S. authorities for smuggling aliens and contraband across the Niagara River into the United States via railway cars. He was eventually acquitted of the charges in U.S. Federal Court, but still lost his job with the railway.[15] O'Leary's chief defence had been that the charges were the result of a frame-up, due to his diligent efforts in fighting liquor smuggling.[16] It certainly is possible that O'Leary, as a newcomer to the Michigan Central, began disrupting the status quo of the smugglers and bootleggers that were quite common to the area at the time, and that they had set him up.

Prohibition was in full force in the U.S. at that time, and liquor exporting and smuggling into the U.S. from Canada was big business. One thing is certain: A pattern in O'Leary's life seems to have emerged, with him going from one job to the next, seeking adventure, excitement, and sometimes even danger.

During his tenures as both a temperance officer and a railway detective, O'Leary would have seen firsthand how financially lucrative bootlegging and smuggling could be, especially in south Niagara along the river and westward along the north shore of Lake Erie. The financial temptations would have been enormous for a man in his position. Everyone was doing it.

In the spring of 1925, after his dismissal from the railway and prior to his appointment as chief of police in Crystal Beach, O'Leary began conducting "dry raids" for liquor in the Crystal Beach area. This was on his own time, prior to actually having been sworn in as a Crystal Beach police officer.[17]

If indeed O'Leary was kicking in doors and entering premises, presumably armed, with the same intensity and ferocity that he had displayed while attacking German machine gun nests, one can only imagine the shock and outright terror that the targets of these raids experienced.

Perhaps he thought he was "auditioning" for the job of police chief. Whether he was just getting an early start on his duties in Crystal Beach, or whether he was illegally seizing liquor from bootleggers under the guise of being a police officer is lost to history. Two things, however, are certain: O'Leary was not a police officer at the time of his raids, and none of the liquor seized in these raids was ever turned in or accounted for.[18] It was alleged at the time that O'Leary had been associated in this criminal enterprise by an individual named Al Moen.[19]

Hopefully, the Crystal Beach village council was unaware of O'Leary's activities (both with the Michigan Central and in Crystal Beach) prior to them hiring him as chief of police. Perhaps George Pinkerton's abrupt dismissal and O'Leary's immediate hiring was a sincere effort by the village council to crack down on the bootlegging activity in the area. George Pinkerton's termination was very sudden, and the war hero O'Leary's immediate appointment thereafter, was hailed in the media as the coming of the saviour.

Prior to his appointment as chief constable in Crystal Beach becoming effective on July 1, 1925, one such raid O'Leary had conducted was on the home of a wealthy Buffalo businessman, who was a summer resident in the Crystal Beach area. It was reported that the businessman had paid the individual named Al Moen $750 (over $10,000 in today's funds) for "services rendered," but apparently Moen did not fulfill whatever his end of the agreement had been.[20]

When a complaint was made by the gentleman, the OPP were advised, and it was discovered that O'Leary had not reported the raid to anyone, nor had the seized liquor ever been turned in or accounted for. It could be assumed that O'Leary and Moen were co-conspirators in the bogus raids, and only got caught once the victim complained about being duped out of his liquor and his $750.

On September 4, 1925, on orders from the Ontario Attorney General, O'Leary was arrested and charged with impersonating an officer, having conducted his "raids" prior to his appointment as chief of police having taken effect.[21] Further charges were pending against O'Leary and Moen in regards to the non-reporting and disappearance of the liquor which had been seized. As was the case in the police/liquor scandal five months earlier in Port Colborne, authorities would not comment on the investigation. No information was released on O'Leary's relationship with Al Moen, or about the missing liquor and money.[22]

As a result of the OPP's investigation into O'Leary, a provincial inquiry into "Rum-Running" and bootlegging activities in the Crystal Beach area was ordered by T.D. Cowper, Crown Attorney of Welland

County. The federal Department of Justice was also brought in to the investigation.[23]

It appears that the Crystal Beach vigilance group's complaints in the early 1950s had some historical validity to them. At the time, liquor and human smuggling from Canada into the United States was a hugely profitable business, as O'Leary had learned during his days as a temperance officer, and even more so as a railroad detective with Michigan Central.

During U.S. Prohibition, despite the Ontario Temperance Act, cross-border smuggling and legal exportation was very active and lucrative from the Niagara River westward as far as Port Colborne, Port Maitland, Long Point, and on down to Windsor. As mentioned in the previous chapter, in 1930 legal liquor exports alone accounted for one fifth of total federal revenue, generating more revenue than even income tax.[24] The profits on the illegal side of things were probably even greater.

The eastern end of Lake Erie narrows considerably, and this area, especially Port Colborne, was therefore much more conducive to making quick runs across to the U.S. shore, as opposed to further west in the middle of the lake, where it widens out to more than sixty miles.

On July 2 1925, just one day after Michael O'Leary's appointment as Crystal Beach's chief of police took effect, and just after Chief Frank Reavley's dismissal at Port Colborne, Canadian authorities, along with U.S. Customs, seized a large cruiser and six launches in the harbour at Port Colborne, Ontario. The amount seized was $25,000 worth of whiskey (worth over $300,000 today), along with 350 cases of beer. Most of the contraband had been stolen from boxcars in the railway sidings in Port Colborne and loaded onto the boats, bypassing the legal export process. The freight cars and their contents belonged to the shadowy Port Colborne liquor-exporting group known as the "syndicate."[25]

As stated in the previous chapter, whether Rocco Perri was associated with the Port Colborne liquor syndicate or not, this theft was likely committed either from him, or by him.

In 1925 in Port Colborne, when an incident involving huge loads of liquor being stolen from train cars and smuggled it into the United States, Rocco Perri would no doubt have had at least some prior knowledge of a theft of this much liquor. As previously mentioned, he had many civil servants and lawmen on his payroll, in addition to an associate connected to Port Colborne.

O'Leary's illegal dry-raid activities in the Crystal Beach area during the weeks prior to his appointment, the disappearance of the contraband seized in these raids, his previous experience with the railroad and its security procedures, along with his previous involvement and arrest for smuggling, all raise many questions. Would O'Leary have somehow been peripherally involved, or have had prior knowledge of this massive attempted liquor theft and smuggling operation thwarted on July 2 in Port Colborne?

It is strange that two future Crystal Beach police chiefs, Frank Reavley and Michael O'Leary, had both worked in many different capacities right in the middle of all of this illicit liquor, bootlegging, and smuggling activity in the southern Niagara Peninsula prior to their days in Crystal Beach. No doubt they were both well aware of the money people were making by taking part in it.

It is no wonder that, in 1927, the federal government opened a Royal Commission into Customs and Excise in the Golden Horseshoe region. The government was well aware of Al Capone and his associates south of the border, and that he was one of the chief consumers of the products "exported" from Canada.

After his arrest, O'Leary was remanded into custody for more than a month in the Welland County jail awaiting his hearing, which was held at the Municipal Hall in Crystal Beach. The provincial and federal inquiries were still running their course when Michael O'Leary was ultimately acquitted of the personation charge. The disposition of the inquiry into the seized liquor and money was never publicly disclosed. O'Leary was dismissed from his job as chief of police in Crystal Beach, having lasted only two months and three days in that position. It was an inglorious departure for the world-famous war hero.

O'Leary's predecessor, George Pinkerton, who was so unceremoniously dumped by the village council in June 1925, was reinstated as police chief, and held the job until September 1928. He made the news for arresting Buffalo Police officer Charles Cogan on a public intoxication charge in Crystal Beach on the Fourth of July weekend in 1928.

It was reported that Pinkerton had to resort to using his billystick to subdue Cogan, who was found guilty and fined fifty dollars plus costs at his hearing in the Ridgeway municipal courthouse.[26] Pinkerton maintained a relatively low profile, appearing in the media for things such as being involved in the approval of a dance marathon in the Crystal Ballroom in July of 1928.[27]

He was also cited in an article in the media regarding reported upcoming liquor raids by the OPP in the Crystal Beach area, no doubt arising out of the provincial and federal inquiries into bootlegging in the Crystal Beach area after the O'Leary arrest.[28]

In the spring of 1926, months after his acquittal from the Crystal Beach charges, Michael John O'Leary applied for a job with the City of Hamilton as a sanitary inspector.[29] It is unlikely that he was successful in this application process, as by October, 1926 he had applied for welfare relief from the City of Hamilton to secure fare back to Ireland for the family. O'Leary claimed that he had a wealthy uncle there who would take care of them. However, it was reported that O'Leary remained in Ontario, working with the Attorney General's office, while only his wife and family returned home.[30]

Michael John O'Leary left no fewer than seven jobs during his time in Canada. Eventually returning to England and re-joining his family with the help of the British Legion, he worked for them in their poppy factory, and also as a commissionaire at the Mayfair Hotel. On November 9, 1929, along with three to four hundred other Victoria Cross recipients, O'Leary attended a ceremonial dinner in their honour which was attended by the Prince of Wales.[31]

After World War Two broke out, O'Leary, now in his forties, rejoined the military, once again seeking the thrill and excitement that he seemed to crave. He was assigned as a Captain to the Middlesex

Regiment and joined the British Expeditionary Force in France, before being sent back to Britain as a result of a flare-up of his malaria. He then ran a prisoner-of-war facility in southern England.[32]

In 1945, Michael John O'Leary, VC, was discharged from the military due to medical disability with the rank of Major, and went on to work as a building contractor. He attended many Remembrance Day ceremonies and parades over the years, and countless stories, articles and photos of him are available on the internet. Whatever had happened over in Canada, Michael O'Leary is still idolized as a legitimate war hero in the U.K., especially in Ireland.

Michael O'Leary's medals at Irish Guard's R.H.Q., London.

Photo: Thomas Stewart

Major Michael John O'Leary VC, war hero, former Mountie, Ontario Provincial Police Officer, and one-time Chief of Police of the Village of Crystal Beach, Ontario, died two months before his seventieth birthday in the Whittington Hospital in Islington, England on August 1, 1961.

Because of his connections to Canada, he is memorialized across the country at several locations: the Barrie Military Heritage Park, the Victoria Cross Memorial in York Cemetery in Toronto, the RCMP Training Depot in Regina, Saskatchewan, and on the Veterans Affairs Canada website. Today, his exploits of courage are the subject of study in some American and Irish college and university Irish Studies programs.

Oddly, and also unfortunately, in Crystal Beach, Ontario, where he was once celebrated as the saviour of the police department and the scourge of bootleggers, Michael John O'Leary, war hero and Victoria Cross recipient, is completely forgotten to history.

Since the 1890s, a lot of tough guys have walked the streets of Crystal Beach, including John Lacey, the Giant Terror of Crystal Beach, heavyweight champion Joe Louis, the Outlaws Motorcycle Club, Police Chief Floyd Garrard, mobsters, prizefighters, professional wrestlers, and many legendary locals. However, Michael John O'Leary, V.C., despite his misgivings, is undoubtedly the biggest badass who ever set foot in the Village of Crystal Beach.

Michael O'Leary V. C. Memorial, RCMP Training Depot, Regina, Saskatchewan.

Photo: Dan Pooler

CHAPTER SEVEN:
THE VAUDEVILLIANS

Crystal Beach Park had a long history as an entertainment centre from the late 1800s right up until it closed in 1989. When the original midway started growing along the Oak Ridge, theatres and tents were erected, with shows as diverse as escape acts and Japanese acrobats. The outdoor shows were more daring-do thrill shows, such as aerialists and high divers, but the tents and theatres along the midway featured many performers who had once graced vaudeville stages across the United States. Some of them stayed in Crystal Beach, just as some professional wrestlers had chosen to do, and some went back to travelling the vaudeville circuit, returning to the Beach for the summers. At one time, there was even an area of Crystal Beach known as the "Actor's Colony."[1]

In the early days, bands and orchestras would play outdoors on the north side of the dune, which had crude wooden bleachers built into it, forming a primitive amphitheatre. Then came the dance pavilion along the midway. In 1925, live musical entertainment in Crystal Beach entered its golden age with the construction of the Crystal Ballroom. The venue hosted some of the top big bands and orchestras in the world: The Dorsey Brothers orchestras, Gene Krupa, Artie Shaw, and Count Basie are just a few of the performers who appeared at the Crystal Beach Ballroom.

Omer and Ruth Hébert, a veteran vaudeville couple from the United States, arrived in Crystal Beach the opposite way, settling there after two decades on the top theatrical circuits across the United States. After twenty-plus years on the road, the Héberts retired and settled in Crystal Beach, opened a hotel, and ultimately left a lasting legacy to the community.

Vaudeville refers to a variety show style of theatrical performance, which started in Europe and became popular in North America from the late 1800s until the 1930s. A vaudeville show was an accessible form of entertainment for people from all walks of life and social status, as tickets were affordable for most people. The entertainment was generally kept clean, with no nudity, swearing, or smoking allowed—as opposed to the more risqué Burlesque circuit. Racial segregation was a daily and nightly reality on the American vaudeville circuit.

Ruth Wilkinson Hébert was born in Warsaw, New York on August 29, 1890 to Hattie Crossman and John Wilkinson.[2]

In the 1900 U.S. Census for Buffalo, Erie County, Ruth's mother Hattie was widowed and had moved to Buffalo when Ruth was young.[3] Perhaps, when she lived in Buffalo as a young girl, Ruth Wilkinson had once visited Crystal Beach, and the pleasant memories drew her back there years later when she retired from the vaudeville circuit. It is an endearing thought.

Wilfred "Omer" Hébert was born in 1887 in Quebec.[4] He emigrated to the United States in 1905 at age eighteen. Omer made his living in New York and Chicago as a professional musician, musical director, and band leader.

By 1910, Ruth and Omer were working together in New York State regional theatres and on the northeast vaudeville circuit. They played wherever the shows took them, including some of the fanciest and grandest theatres in the eastern United States. Omer was the band leader and Ruth was the singer, dancer, actress, and saxophone player.

Omer had one of the most popular jazz bands in the New York State area at the time, Omer Hébert's Girly Jazzy Revue. Ruth was often billed as "America's premier dancer."[5] She initially used her mother's maiden name, billed as Ruth Crossman, but after her marriage she was billed under her married name, Ruth Hébert.

She received rave reviews across the country, extolling her singing voice, her dancing, and her prowess on the saxophone.

In *The Cohocton N.Y. Valley Times*: "They carry a full orchestra, a prima donna, Miss Ruth Crossman, who has a voice of great purity and strength" (22 Sept. 1920).[6]

In *The Wayland Register*: "Miss Ruth Crossman, America's premier dancer, is with Omer Hébert's Revue" (9 Sep. 1920).[7]

In the *Plattsburgh Daily Press*: "Hear the Saxophone Sextet and the Male Quartet, A Musical Cocktail of Jazzy Music That Will Intoxicate You with Joy Headed by Miss Ruth Crossman, America's Premier Dancer and Her Jazz Boys" (29 Jun. 1920).[9]

And in the *Hornell Evening Tribune Times*:

> Another member of this company, Miss Ruth Crossman is a noted saxophone artist and introduces while playing the instrument many difficult dancing steps. Miss Crossman comes from the vaudeville ranks and is a very clever woman in her diversified lines. She has youth, beauty, personality, a pretty figure, a wonderful sweet soprano voice with no coloratura effects, a clear enunciation, one clearly hearing every word she sings in all parts of the theatre. Combined with being a dancer of note as well as an artist on the saxophone, and in all her work a finished artist, she is a remarkable find for Hébert. (22 Sep. 1920)[8]

Ruth was once described in the media as the world's foremost Tango specialist.[10] She and Omer travelled the United States, playing on the Loew's, Keith, Pantages, and Western Vaudeville circuits, appearing on the same bill with many of the popular African American jazz bands and musicians of the day. Vaudeville shows themselves were not segregated, as black performers did appear on the circuit, and audience members were an integrated mix. However, in that era, the performers and bands themselves were segregated on stage. The acts could advertise on the same bill, but could not appear on stage together. You were either a "black" jazz band or a "white" jazz band. Mixed-race line-ups were forbidden.

On their own time, however, the performers were allowed to gather for jam sessions after hours and between shows.[11] In the 1920s, African Americans had assigned areas that they could go to, but nowhere else. Ruth and Omer were undoubtedly firsthand witnesses to this systemic segregation for more than two decades. They knew firsthand the effects that it had on their friends and fellow jazz artists. Their African American friends would have to use separate accommodations, restaurants, bathrooms, even transportation.

Ruth and Omer spent the 1920s touring with many brilliant African American musicians whom they admired and respected, but with whom they were not allowed to appear on stage, or have dinner with, or share accommodations with. The black performers on the circuit, some of the best jazz and ragtime players in the world, could not even stay in the same hotel, sometimes having to sleep on the bus. To survive in their chosen profession, Ruth and Omer would have been obligated to grudgingly accept the unwritten rules of the circuit. This experience more than likely affected them deeply, as would be reflected years later in Ruth's will, after she passed away.

In the mid-1910s, the Héberts were working the New York City area vaudeville scene. Omer also worked as a musical director for Le Comte and Flesher out of Chicago, travelling to produce and perform the music for various theatrical shows and productions.

For perspective, this was around the same time that another future Crystal Beach resident, Michael John O'Leary, was performing his heroic deeds on the battlefield in World War One. As seen in the previous chapter, O'Leary would also follow his own celebrated, yet questionable, path to Crystal Beach.

In 1918, Ruth and Omer were married and Omer was drafted into the U.S. Army. He too headed for service in World War One. He served in France and held the rank of Band Sergeant with the 365th Field Artillery.[12] He was in France for only five months, but he was obviously

CRYSTAL BEACH: OUT OF THE PARK

inspired by the courage of his fellow soldiers. When he returned to the United States, Omer produced and performed the music for one of the biggest live photoplays of its day, *The Lost Battalion*, which chronicled and honoured the men lost or killed in the Battle of Argonne.

A photoplay was a theatrical show of projected images or moving pictures telling a story set to the music of a live orchestra. Some involved on-stage performances with live actors and performers interacting with the images. It was a moving, spectacular production featuring many of the actual men who fought at Argonne, narrating passages from their own experiences. In 2001, a movie was made called *The Lost Battalion*, starring Ricky Schroder, chronicling the famous event.

The Héberts toured other vaudeville circuits out of state and across the northeast, playing date after date, sometimes two shows a day, then on to the next theatre in the next town.

The faded and grainy 101-year-old newspaper photo below is likely the only existing photo of Ruth and Omer on stage together.

Omer Hébert, Ruth Hébert, Burt Peck at the Shattuck Theatre, Hornell, New York, 1920.

Photo: Hornell Evening Tribune-Times

Around 1929, after twenty tough years of life on the road, Omer and Ruth Hébert left show business and settled in Crystal Beach, Ontario. Life on the vaudeville circuit was not easy, and it became even tougher once "talkies" started replacing vaudeville as America's preferred form of theatrical entertainment. Soon, the main features became the moving pictures, and the vaudeville performers became the opening or side acts. It was a tough existence, but it must have been an incredibly romantic journey for the two of them.

Ruth and Omer had never stopped touring long enough to have children and raise a family, as music and entertaining had been their chosen path. In Crystal Beach, they acquired a small building on Ridgeway Road that they called the Hébert's Inn, then moved one door north to a large beautiful building at 10 Ridgeway Road. They named it the Hébert Hotel on the roadside sign, and Hotel Hébert on the building sign. In the 40s it became the Hébert Tavern, then changed drastically over the years through numerous additions and renovations.

The Hébert Hotel, circa 1930s.

Photo: Courtesy Shawn Moore

The hotel was a respectable place—by Crystal Beach standards—modelled in the style of a night club with a beautiful terrazzo floor in the lobby. They had their name—with the accent over the letter "e"—inlaid in the lobby floor tiles. The Starlight Room was the name of the lounge, which occasionally featured live entertainment.

Alcohol was banned in Ontario under the Ontario Temperance Act from 1916 until 1927. When the Héberts arrived in the Beach in 1929, Crystal Beach had just been through the Michael O'Leary incident, and a provincial crackdown on bootlegging in the Crystal Beach area had just taken place. It can be reasonably assumed that the Héberts had heard the local stories about O'Leary, the previous police chief, and other sordid tales of Crystal Beach bootlegging.

Although drinking liquor in public establishments remained illegal for several more years, the Héberts were more than likely hoping to obtain a much-coveted liquor licence for their new place. In the early 1930s, the Lincoln Hotel in Crystal Beach received one of the first liquor licences in Ontario. Licences for beer and wine started being issued in 1934.

The Héberts appear to have been straight shooters, and they ran a reputable business. The couple immediately became involved in the community, donating a room at their establishment for the Ridgeway-Crystal Beach Kinsmen Club to hold their meetings in. Omer joined the Ridgeway Lions Club and was a member of Branch 230 of the Royal Canadian Legion. They sponsored many sports teams in the area, and Ruth would often serve lunch at the hotel for the churchgoers after the Sunday services at St. George's Church just up the road.

Sometimes Ruth would play the piano in the lobby of the hotel, just to make people happy, or perhaps just to re-live the old days. They really came to love Crystal Beach, and became part of the fabric of their adopted hometown.

In their later years, the Héberts hired Jimmy Iezzi and his wife Doris to manage the hotel, while Ruth and Omer retired to their residence above the business.

Jimmy Iezzi, Manager of Hotel Hébert.

Photo: Larry and Elaine Culling

In November of 1949, Omer passed away at home from a sudden heart attack. Three years later, in October of 1952, Ruth passed away at Douglas Memorial Hospital in Fort Erie. They had no children and left no survivors. And this is where the story gets interesting.

In her will, Ruth Hébert bequeathed $5000 (equivalent to $52,000 in today's currency) to the Ridgeway-Crystal Beach Kinsmen Club to be used to purchase playground space for children. In her will, she specified that such a space be "open to children of the area of all races and creeds at no charge."[13] That was an exceptionally progressive statement to make in one's will back in 1952. It raises the question of what motivated her choice of words. Was this phrase written by Ruth because of the segregation she and Omer had witnessed while on the vaudeville circuit? For whatever reason, it was in her heart to set something very inclusive and positive into motion for the entire community. Crystal Beach village reeve Claude Brewster proposed at the time that such a park be named "Hébert Memorial Playground." At one time there was a Hébert Park in Crystal Beach at Belfast and Lincoln Roads. However, Ruth and her name were forgotten over the years, and the small park was re-named Madeline Faiazza Memorial Park in 2007 by the Town of Fort Erie.

Dancer's Legacy For Playground

CRYSTAL BEACH, Ont. (CP)— The will of a one-time dancer who owned a hotel here provides $5,000 for a playground to be set up in the village.

Mrs. Ruth Hebert, who at the time of her death operated the Hotel Hebert, specified in her will that the playground must be open to children of the area "of all races and creeds and at no charge."

Mrs. Hebert, a native of Warsaw N. Y., was well known in her younger days as a dancer, singer and actress.

Reeve Claude Brewster said a name proposed for the area is Hebert Memorial Playground.

Canadian Press, 1952

There is another possible explanation for Ruth's inclusion of the words "all races and creeds" in the wording of her will. Ruth's mother, Hattie Crossman, was born in 1861 in Genesee County, New York. She married John Wilkinson, and Ruth was born in Warsaw, New York in 1890. By 1900, Hattie was no longer with John. The 1900 U.S. Census for Buffalo and Erie County lists Hattie Crossman as the head of the household at 119 Division Street in Buffalo. The census clearly lists Hattie Wilkinson's entry under the "race or color" column with the letter "b," which at the time meant "black." Ruth and her brother are both listed with a letter "b," which appears to have then be overwritten by a letter "w" beside both of the children.[14]

If Ruth's mother Hattie Crossman was indeed African American, or even mixed-race, Ruth would have no doubt witnessed her mother experience the same things that she and Omer had seen on the vaudeville circuit. Whatever was behind the words Ruth chose, she was making a powerful and specific statement.

Of course, any genealogical speculation is impossible to verify short of a DNA test, but it certainly adds an additional layer of mystery and intrigue to Ruth's motivation for bringing the word "race" into her will at a time when segregation was actually still in existence in the U.S.

Another explanation is that it just as likely could have been a simple mistake on the part of the census-taker, which was not uncommon at the time. In fact, in the 1905 U.S. Census, Hattie (now McGuire) is listed as the wife of Henry McGuire, an Irishman, who was her former boarder from the 1900 census. Henry McGuire is now listed as Head of the Household, and thus would have been providing the answers to the census taker. The other family members, including Hattie, are designated as "w" in the "race or color" column.[15]

Although at one time the village had designated the tiny plot of land at Belfast and Lincoln "Hébert Park", it was not actually purchased by the Kinsmen with Ruth's bequest, as it was already village property. In 1959, the Kinsmen, after a great deal of addition fundraising combined with Ruth's bequest, purchased sixteen acres of land on Rebstock Road in order to properly honour her final wishes.

The bequest from Ruth Hébert set in motion a two decade-long chain of events that eventually resulted in what exists on that plot of land today, the Crystal Ridge Community Centre. The complex includes an arena, a library, a playground, a football field, basketball and tennis courts, a splash pad, and most importantly, open space for "children of all races and creeds" to play.

In 1965, the Kinsmen purchased the abandoned St. George Church building on Ridgeway Road—where the new fire hall was built in 1965—and moved it to the Rebstock Road property, converting it into the Crystal Beach Community Centre in 1967. It was there that the Kinsmen built the area's first incarnation of a public "arena." It was a full-size outdoor hockey rink, complete with boards and nets, and it was always busy.

On weekends, teen dances would be held inside the hall. Teenagers in Crystal Beach, like thousands of others across North America had recently seen the Beatles on television, and Beatlemania was in full swing. Every teenage male wanted an electric guitar and an amplifier. Some wanted drums. Everyone's hair got longer. As a result, garage bands started popping up all across North America, and Crystal Beach was no different.

In Crystal Beach and Ridgeway, bands with names like The Surfers, The Rogues, The Dissociation and The New Breed would pack the Crystal Beach Community Centre on weekends. In the 60s, the matching suits and outfits of the band members, along with John Lennon-style Pea Caps were just as important as the music. Cover versions of British Invasion hits, mostly Beatles, along with old R&B standards, were the usual setlists of the day.

Sadly, the Crystal Beach Community Centre burned down in 1971, and the land was offered up for sale by the Kinsmen to the Town of Fort Erie for one dollar, with the offer conditional upon an arena being built on the property within two years of transfer.[16]

The common theme amongst all parties throughout the decades following the securing of this parcel of land and subsequent land transfers, was to always keep it free of development and for recreational use, maintaining the spirit of Ruth Hébert's final wishes. There were occasional rumours and proposals of housing developments, and also for a school to be built on various parts of the property, but they were always met with resistance from the community, most of whom weren't even aware of Ruth Hébert's will from 1952. But deep inside, they somehow did know.

In November 1974, after many more fund drives and much hard work by the Ridgeway Lions Club, the Kinsmen Club, and scores of community-minded volunteers, the $640,000 West End Arena was opened.

Mayor Teal and the Kinsmen both called it "a 20-year dream come true."[17] The majority of the funding for construction and property costs came from the Town of Fort Erie. Further funding came from the Lion's Club ($100,000), the Kinsmen Club ($20,000, plus the property and a Zamboni), federal and provincial grants, and public subscription.[18] The Ridgeway Lions Club took the lead from there, and they continue to manage the facility today as the recreational hub of the community.

The Crystal Ridge Community Centre, with its roots going back to a 1952 gift from a retired American vaudevillian, is now a place that the entire community can enjoy. Hopefully, Reeve Claude Brewster's original 1952 proposal for the name Hébert Memorial Park will one day adorn this property in some capacity, recognizing the gift that Omer and Ruth left to their adopted community.

This newspaper photo from 1919 is one of the few photos of Ruth Hébert from her Vaudeville stage career.

Photo: *The Buffalo Courier*

Chapter Eight:
The Circus Leaves Town

The closing of Crystal Beach Amusement Park in 1989 had a devastating effect on the village and the people in it. It broke the hearts of millions of people who still held the place near and dear. Expectedly, the decline of the park in its final years mirrored the decline of the village at the same time. More recently, however, Crystal Beach is once again booming and experiencing a renaissance as a summer beach destination.

Crystal Beach welcome sign.

Photo: Author

There are too many theories and opinions as to why the park closed to list them all. One thing is certain: The closure and sale of the park still raises a lot of emotional responses from people both in casual conversation, and on social media group pages. Books have been written about it. Jennifer Wismer wrote her Master's thesis on the subject, and it is available through the National Library of Canada. Her work is cited within this book.

Cutting through all of the opinions, theories, and emotions, there are certain benchmark events that had significant impacts on park attendance over the years, and its eventual demise. Cumulatively, and combined within each other, along with the evolving market conditions of those times, all of these factors impacted the park throughout the years, leading up to its closure in 1989.

The Comet, after the park's closing, 1989.

Photo: Cathy Herbert

In 1927 the Peace Bridge was built. The *Canadiana* and the *Americana* lost passengers, resulting in the sale of the *Americana* in 1929. Prior to the bridge, other than the steamers, visitors from Buffalo could cross at the ferry crossing in Fort Erie, then travel by train, bus or buggy to Crystal Beach. Although the park gained visitors by car from Buffalo, a single automobile would only bring four or five people at the most, and Crystal Beach's tiny village streets became congested with cars that were now parking everywhere. When three thousand people crossed the lake on the *Canadiana*, they were all going to one place and one place only, and usually for the whole day. They also paid boat fare to the company. Three thousand people crossing the Peace Bridge by car not only eliminated potential boat revenue, it also made it possible for those three thousand people to go somewhere else, instead of Crystal Beach.

The automobile and the bridge gave Western New Yorkers, the park's largest base of customers, the opportunity to bypass Crystal Beach and travel further on to explore other tourist destinations such as Niagara Falls and Toronto. This change in demographics wasn't a devastating blow to business, but it was the first of many challenges to the park's antiquated and, shall we say, "fragile" business model.

The *Canadiana*, which brought three thousand people on each run, discontinued its service after the huge fight on board in May of 1956. The end of the ferry service certainly cut into, and dramatically changed the demographic of the customer base for the park. On Labour Day 1956, the Captain of the *Canadiana* took his traditional stroll through the park, then set sail from Crystal Beach for the last time. He anchored the boat offshore, and a fireworks show from the top of the ship was seen by all from Crystal Beach to Buffalo. The onboard orchestra played "Auld Lang Syne." Then, the *Canadiana* sailed off into the night, becoming just another Crystal Beach memory. After years of failed efforts to restore the vessel, all that was eventually salvaged of the ship was the propellor, the capstan, and the bollard.

These items were rescued and refurbished by locals Rick Doan, Paul Kassay, and Harvey Holzworth, with the help of many other volunteers. The items now sit on display at Crystal Beach's Waterfront Park, in full view of the *Canadiana*'s former route across Lake Erie. Both landing points of the *Canadiana*, in Buffalo and Crystal Beach, are visible from the display's location.

The Canadiana propellor and capstan, overlooking her old route.

Photo: Author

In 1960, Fantasy Island opened on Grand Island, New York, giving amusement park enthusiasts yet another alternative to Crystal Beach.

It's odd, but the residents of Crystal Beach actually lost their village long before they lost their amusement park. The park actually outlived the village by eighteen years.

On January 1, 1971, the clock struck midnight for the last time in the Village of Crystal Beach. It ceased to exist as a political entity, and was amalgamated into the Town of Fort Erie, along with Bertie Township and Stevensville. Municipal and regional government took over, and the lucrative tax revenue arrangement that the village enjoyed for years with the Crystal Beach Company came to an abrupt end.

The park's municipal taxes would now go to the Town of Fort Erie, and the Region of Niagara. Goodbye to local sidewalk and street repairs by the village crews. Crystal Beach now had to get in line with the rest of the once-independent communities within the new Town of Fort Erie for local services, upgrades, and improvements. Once the village closed shop, any issues within the former village boundaries became the concern of the town, or the region.

The park owners would now be dealing with the Town of Fort Erie council, as opposed to their old friends on Crystal Beach village council. It would be fascinating to unravel how the park's financial dealings with the new government differed from the cozy and longtime arrangement they once had with the village. The new "business arrangement" would no doubt be cutting into the Hall's traditional profit margin.

While the political existence of Crystal Beach came to an abrupt end, the economic state of the village mirrored the park's gradual decline until it closed in 1989. As the park got shabbier and shabbier, businesses in the village started boarding up windows.

The 1973 oil crisis was actually much worse than the 1979 crisis. Gas prices were much higher in '73. Automobiles and busses had become the two main modes of transport for amusement park guests, and many people just weren't driving that summer. Without ferry service to deliver guests, this seriously reduced park attendance that year.

In 1976, park management implemented a general admission fee and policy for the park. It was universally despised, especially by the locals and the summer cottagers. It put an end to people casually visiting the park for a ride or two and a Hall's sucker. There would be no more just walking into the park for an evening stroll, or hanging out on a bench to people-watch, or munch on a sugar waffle.

In fact, management even got rid of the benches. Guests were basically committed to paying a general admission price, then spending the entire day and/or evening in the park in order to get their money's worth. Tickets were no longer required except for the featured rides like the Comet. This new policy eliminated local and casual visitors and changed the dynamic of the park's clientele even more. Many people feel that the general admission decision was a disaster.

In 1981, the park faced some real challenges attracting visitors. It was the year that both Darien Lake Fun Country in New York State, and Canada's Wonderland north of Toronto opened. The park's Buffalo customers and large company picnics could now go to Darien Lake, without having to cross the border. Many Canadian customers from the Golden Horseshoe area were lost to Canada's Wonderland.

Large theme parks were rapidly displacing traditional North American amusement parks. Expansion was out of the question, as

Crystal Beach Park, at a fixed thirty-seven acres, simply did not have the available area to compete with the huge new parks. Two years later, the amusement park went into receivership and was operated by Ramsi Tick on behalf of the receiver.

In 1984, the park was purchased by a group of private owners, including former owner Ed Hall, along with Buffalo attorney Joseph Biondolillo, and Rudy Bonifacio, whose father John Bonifacio had run J. B. Concessions at Crystal Beach since the mid-60s. They made a final attempt at reviving (some say rescuing) the park, with television ad campaigns, indoor concerts in the Crystal Ballroom, and outdoor shows by the new beach club, Schooners. Despite Schooners always being packed, for some unknown reason it leaked money like a sieve. The park even hosted the Diet Pepsi Crystal Beach Triathlon, won by Joel Sprague of Buffalo. The race drew over 200 competitors from Western New York and Southern Ontario.

In spite of all the new promotions, there was still a sense around the village that the park's days were numbered. Biondolillo's dismantling and pieced-off auction sale of the magnificent Crystal Beach carousel was seen by many as the final nail in the lid of the park's future.

On Labour Day 1989, Crystal Beach Amusement Park closed its gates for the last time, breaking the hearts of millions and rendering the park nothing but a memory. An auction of the rides and amusements took place on a cold rainy day in October, 1989.

For a while, after everything was sold or removed, the entire 37-acre property just sat vacant, devoid of life or activity. It was a melancholy experience to drive by and see the shocking contrast from just a year earlier, when that same space had been the heart of a community. It was as if a giant malevolent hand had reached down out of the sky and wrenched away the heart, the spirit, and the roots of the community's past. The property was purchased by a real estate development group and today the Crystal Beach Yacht and Tennis Club stands where the park used to be.

CRYSTAL BEACH: OUT OF THE PARK

December 24, 1989, three months after closing.

Photo: Cathy Herbert

Once the park closed, the Beach became a desolate ghost town, with many boarded-up businesses that had once depended on the summer tourists and park goers. Hundreds of people lost jobs that they had held for decades. Hundreds of students would now have to look for summer jobs outside of the village. The summer air was silent. There were no more miniature train whistles, or screams of terror from the roller coasters. Eleven p.m. would come and go in silence, unnoticed, as the park's closing whistle no longer sounded across the village.

There have been a lot of ill feelings about the park closing. Some people accuse the developers of greed, while others allege poor management on the part of the park owners. Regardless, accusations and allegations aren't the same as facts. Lost in the emotion over a beloved amusement park closing, is the devastating socio-economic and financial impact that an entire community suffered through. Some families had been third and fourth generation park employees. These were the people hit the hardest and most affected by the closure.

Perhaps the traditional old-school American amusement park had simply seen its better days, just like the old-school village system of government. Even so, the huge new theme parks may be bigger, shinier, and more orderly, but none of them will ever match the mid-century American feel of the Crystal Beach Amusement Park.

Where the Crystal Beach Amusement Park once stood.

Photo: Author

Situated where the amusement park once was, the Crystal Beach Yacht and Tennis Club is an attractive gated community, with access to the beach for its residents. Its existence raises a gamut of mixed emotions amongst fans of the old amusement park, and varied opinions amongst locals and historians. Some resent it and call it the "vinyl village." Others feel that it's much better than having an abandoned amusement park or empty lot sitting there. Others still believe that somehow, some charitable soul should have stepped in and magically kept a money-losing venture going well past its money-making days.

Today, the only reminder that Crystal Beach Amusement Park was even there is a plaque at the corner of Erie and Ridgeway Roads, commemorating the private enclave as the site where the park once stood. The founder, John E. Rebstock, is mentioned in passing on the plaque. It states that his "success in establishing a religious campground in 1888 brought prosperity to the area," but in fact, it was his success in the resort and real estate business which brought prosperity to the area, following two failed attempts at establishing a religious campground.

CRYSTAL BEACH: OUT OF THE PARK

Photo: Author

The population of the village changed gradually after the park closed, as well as the social fabric of the village, as people changed jobs and drifted apart. Some moved away to find employment. Some stayed, and never found work again. Many families turned to public assistance. Longtime co-workers from the park no longer saw each other every day. It was as if the energy and magic of the amusement park had been an invisible magnetic charge, holding the village together.

There were some dark days, with people wondering if the boards on the storefronts would ever come down again, but over the years the village started slowly coming out of the post-park slump and began a gradual comeback. Real estate became hot again, and the population started to swell, this time with Canadians, and not just for the summer. People started discovering Crystal Beach as a charming little beach community, even without an amusement park.

Several businesses and individuals took chances on the area. Groups like the Crystal Beach Business Improvement Area and the Friends of Crystal Beach have helped restore pride and vitality back into the village.

Real estate and construction are booming, and many new businesses are locating to Crystal Beach. Hot Dog Alley is going through a major renaissance with small businesses, restaurants, and shops replacing the old open-air food stands.

In an eerie similarity to 1921, when John E. Rebstock predicted a building boom in Crystal Beach, it seems to be happening again exactly one hundred years later. Following in the footsteps of John Rebstock in the early 1900s, and later Ted Kassay in the 1970s, local entrepreneur Phil Smith's vision for the revitalization of the village is gaining momentum.

Like the Buffalo Courier Derby over one hundred years ago, there is also once again an annual foot race in the village, the Crystal Beach 5K.

The Crystal Beach BIA has partnered with several other community groups over the years towards the betterment of the village. The Crystal Beach Beautification Committee adorns the streets of the village every spring with incredible flower displays. The Friends of Crystal Beach (FOCB) host an annual Waterfront Concert series within full view of the beautiful lake. The BIA hosts the Thursday food truck concert series. On Saturdays, the Crystal Beach Farmer's Market takes place in the Queens Circle. These groups have spent decades of volunteer hours advancing Crystal Beach, and their efforts are coming to fruition. The Welcome to Crystal Beach sign at the top of the Ridgeway Road hill is an example of their joint efforts, and the story behind its construction and installation is fascinating, and also one of those Crystal Beach tales that still can't be told.

Although not an official village since 1971, Crystal Beach is proving that even without the amusement park, it can stand on its own merits as a beautiful summer resort. People simply love visiting the area, and it is once again becoming the place to be in the summer. The population is different than in the glory days, with the year-round number at around eight thousand people, but the number of summer visitors is much less than the millions during the glory years of the park. The current demographics are very different than the heyday numbers of a thousand residents in the winter, and twenty-five thousand or more in the summer, with thousands more day visitors.

Many retirees from around the Golden Horseshoe are moving to the area. The wild pay parties are gone. There is no longer a flagpole sitter at the top of the hill. There is no official word on the presence of bootleggers, cave hermits, minstrels, or clowns.

The memories still within the millions of people who experienced Crystal Beach even just once, will never be lost. It will always have its quirky and unusual history, from both the park and the village. It will also never lose that beach-town vibe you feel just south of Rebstock Road, where you start seeing sand on the shoulders of the roads.

Hopefully this collection of curious, offbeat, and sometimes gruesome, stories will help document and preserve a thin slice of the village's unique and colourful history.

There is an old saying still used by some longtime Crystal Beachers, both Canadian and American: "Once you get the Crystal Beach sand between your toes, it's there forever." No matter where you go, you will always feel it, and it will always make you want to go back to the Beach.

ABOUT THE AUTHOR

Gary Pooler was born and raised in the Ridgeway-Crystal Beach area. A life-long Crystal Beach resident, he attended Ridgeway-Crystal Beach High School, Western University, and Brock University, receiving a Bachelor's Degree in Psychology.

He worked at Crystal Beach Amusement Park as a brake operator, and later as a lifeguard on Crystal Beach. He also worked for the Bay Beach Corporation, and as a Social Services Caseworker responsible for the Crystal Beach area.

Gary is a retired Ontario Provincial Police officer. He has been a Detective Constable in Organized Crime Enforcement and in Casino Enforcement. He has also held the positions of Intelligence Liaison Officer with the federal government, high school supply teacher, and part-time instructor at Niagara College.

Gary was a member of the Western Mustangs football team, and was drafted by the Montreal Alouettes of the Canadian Football League in 1980. He has also competed in the Hawaiian Ironman Triathlon World Championship. In 2010, he was inducted into the Greater Fort Erie Sports Wall of Fame. He has also coached high school football and track as a community volunteer.

GARY POOLER

Gary lives in Ridgeway with his wife and three teenage sons. Since retiring from the OPP, Gary plays with the Neil Young tribute band, Neo Young. (neoyoung.ca, follow Neo Young on Facebook & You Tube). *"Crystal Beach: Out of the Park"* is his first book.

REEVES
OF CRYSTAL BEACH

George Mathewson	1921
Patrick F. Ryan	1922-1925
J.H. Nagel	1926
Patrick F. Ryan	1927
J.H. Nagel	1928
Patrick F. Ryan	1929-1930
Carl L. Teal	1931-1932
Patrick F. Ryan	1933
Carl L. Teal	1934-1938

Norman L. Smith	1939-1945
Carl L. Teal	1946-1948
Norman L. Smith	1948-1949
Claude Brewster	1950-1955
Frank Shepherd	1956
Jack Millington	1957-1962
Fletcher Teal	1963-1968
Albert Opatovsky Jr.	1969*

*In 1970, the Village of Crystal Beach became part of the Town of Fort Erie. Reeve Opatovsky became the Alderman for the Crystal Beach Ward on the Fort Erie Town Council.

Police Chiefs
of Crystal Beach

Photo: Bob Pyefinch

William Scott	1921
Martin Strauch	1923
George Pinkerton	1923-1925
Michael O'Leary	1925
George Pinkerton	1925-1928
Terrence Burke	1929
Edward Clunie	1929
Frank Reavley/ James Goodall	1929-1941*

Floyd Garrard   1941-1943

L.J. Simpson   1943

Percy Mark   1944-1950

Bernard Kitney   1950

Gilbert Robertson   1950

* The Chief Constable position in Crystal Beach was initially a seasonal job. Later, chiefs were hired on one-year contracts. Some alternated and over-lapped through the position, and some were renewed yearly. Several lasted only weeks or months on the job.

Fire Chiefs
of Crystal Beach

Charles Soper	1921-1925, 1926-27
Martin Strauch	1925-26
W. Brewster	1928-31
W. Bruce	1931-33
H. Lund	1933-38
W. Sloat	1938-42
F. Klauck	1942-47
W. Sloat	1947-48
G. Pietz	1948-54, 1956-59

Vince Teal	1954-56
Amos Taylor	1959-67
Ken Thomson	1967-72*
Howie Climenhaga	1972-1978
Stan Matthews	1978-89
Doug Atkins	1991-2020
R. Lowell	2020

*In 1970, C.B.V.F.D. became Station 6 of the Fort Erie Fire Department.

Sons of Crystal Beach
Who Died in Service of Our Country:

Private Robert James Burd. K.I.A. 19 May 1917, France, WW1.

Warrant Officer John Richard Rebstock. K.I.A. 19 Nov. 1942, Lybia, WW2.

Corporal Albert Hugh Storm. K.I.A. 27 Nov. 2006, Afghanistan.

130 Years

of Crystal Beach Cottage Names

1890S:

Juniper Cottage	Edgewood Cottage
Dunraven	Comfort Cottage
Kenmore	Kilcare Cottage
Beehive	The Robber's Roost
Hickman's Roost	Cedar Cottage
The Pagoda	Forest Home
Tent No. 24	Utopia
Sunshine	Sunny Side
Columbine	Maple Cottage
Buttonwood Villa	Nirvana
Rustic Retreat	Fernwood

EARLY 1900S:

The Cloverleaf	Tangle-Vine
Lincoln Cottage	Contentment
Maple Leaf	The Brooklyn
The Emerson	Iroquois
Grand Jury	Shamrock
Glen Isle	Tara's Hall
Albert	The Buffalo
The Hollywood	The Markeen
Arcadia	St. Josephs Cottage
The Delia	Uncle Tom's Cabin
Crescent	The Coney Island
The Dorien	Susquehanna
Malchen	Green Tree
Rosebud	The Valaria
Gertrude	Buttonwood
Parkview	Pekin
The Buffalo	Tionesta
Villa Santa Barbara	Nodus Tonius

Cook's Villa	Sandy Hook
Swiss Chateau	Fallen Wood
The Orlando	Ma-ru-ka-we
The Cutley	Buena Vista
The Ceck	Hillside Rest
The Augusta	Eagle's Nest
Casa Luma	Wald-heim
Restmore	Evesham
Monrepos	Villa Maria

MID-LATE 1900S:

Suds City	Hotel Sheets
Leper Colony	Handy Caps
Wasted Acres	White Rabbit
Warner Brothers	Ponderosa
L.A.G.N.A.F.	Harvey Wallbanger's
F.U.B.A.R.	Green Tree Inn
D.I.L.L.I.G.A.F.	The Glasgow
S.N.A.F.U.	The Odd Couples
Wrath of Canada	Halfers

Black and Decker	Death Ranch
Magnificent Seven	Peter's Inn
Elmwood Village	Madd Dogs
The Pits	Moose Lodge
The Snake Pit	Bay of Pigs
Purple Lizard	General Hospital
The Mansion	The Harem
Last Resort	Lucky Charms
I Phelta Thigh	Bay of Pigs
Red Caps	The Electric Zipper
The Sewers	Playboy and Playmate
Hard Guys	Fever Zone
F Troop	After Midnight
Umma Gooma	Cuckoo's Nest
The Ballroom	The Wright
Grippers	The New Yorker
Crystal Lodge	Cottage 42
Do Drop Inn	Rose Villa
Rolling Inn	Chateau Flamingo
Tony's Place	

CRYSTAL BEACH: OUT OF THE PARK

If your cottage name is not on this list, I recommend a fine-point gel pen (Author).

ACKNOWLEDGEMENTS

Thank you (alphabetically) to the following people:

Rudy Bonifacio, Owner of Crystal Beach Amusement Park, 1984-1989.
Bob Brown.
Ellen Burd.
Cheryl Fretz Carlyle, Great-grand daughter of John E. Rebstock: family history, photos.
Elaine Culling, Ruth Hébert research.
Larry Culling, photo.
Jerry Deheus, O.P.P. Provincial Constable (Retired).
Dianne Diamond, daughter of Park Police Chief William Diamond.
Rick Doan, photos.
Clark Family, photos.
Ruth and Omer Hébert, inspiration.
Cathy Herbert, photos.
Bill Lee, O.P.P. Sgt. (Retired), volunteer O.P.P. historian.
Stuart McLeod.
Shawn Moore, photos.
Heather Pooler, tolerance.
Tom Tryniski, Old Fulton History newspaper database.
George R. Rebstock, for all the great stories over the years.
Tim Rebstock, Great-grandson of John E. Rebstock: family history, photo.
Gary Sandel, photo of his father John arresting Fifi the Clown.

Mr. White, my Grade 13 English teacher, who once said to me as he returned my morbid and gory creative writing assignment, "You should be writing for True Detective magazine."

SOURCES

CHAPTER ONE SOURCES

1. Niagara Settler's Land Records, Bertie Township Abstracts. A355 #409, sites.google.com/site/niagarasettlers2/bertie-township-abstracts/bertie-map-undated?authuser=0, accessed 27 June 2021.
2. "Life and History of John E. Rebstock, Founder of Crystal Beach". Rebstock, George J. & Helen and Cheryl Fretz Carlyle, 1978.
3. Tim Rebstock, Great-Grandson of John E. Rebstock.
4. "At Crescent Beach". *Buffalo Courier Express*, 17 Aug. 1890, p. 6.
5. Letter of Helen Rebstock.
6. Buffalo Courier, 12 Apr. 1890.
7. "For a Day or Longer". *The Illustrated Buffalo Express*, 31 May 1891.
8. "Crystal Beach Assembly". *Buffalo Evening News*, 13 May, 1895, p. 6.
9. "At Crystal Beach". *The Buffalo Courier*, 13 May 1895, p. 6.
10. Ibid.
11. "Life and History of John E. Rebstock, Founder of Crystal Beach". Rebstock, George J. & Helen, and Cheryl Fretz Carlyle, 1978.
12. Andrews, Peter "Crystal Beach First Opened". *Buffalo Courier Express*, 8 July 1952, p. 13.
13. "At Crystal Beach". *The Buffalo Review*, 19 Aug. 1899, p. 6.
14. "Crystal Beach Opens". *Buffalo Evening News*, 15 June 1896, p. 5.
15. "Buffalo as a Wholesale Point", The Amherst Bee, 25 Feb. 1886.

16. "History of the Campground". www.mvcma.org/history-narrative1.html, accessed 14 June 2021.
17. "Crystal Beach Dominant Summer Resort". *The Tourist Review*, 7 July 1948, Vol. 1 No. 1.
18. "Life and History of John E. Rebstock, Founder of Crystal Beach". Rebstock, George J. & Helen and Cheryl Fretz Carlyle, 1978.
19. web.archive.org/web/20130606184607/http://www.iokds.org/index2.html, accessed 25 June 2021.
20. Baer, Chris "This Was Then: The Cottage City Carnival of 1882". *The Martha's Vineyard Times*, 15 May 2019, /www.mvtimes.com/2019/05/15/cottage-city-carnival-1882-2/ accessed 15 June 2021.
21. "Brief Mention". *The Buffalo Express*, 2 July 1891, p. 5.
22. "Bonfire Illumination at Crystal Bay". Unknown Publication, 12 Aug. 1893.
23. "Crystal Beach". *The Buffalo Courier*, 30 Aug. 1910, p. 10.
24. "Life and History of John E. Rebstock, Founder of Crystal Beach". Rebstock, George J. & Helen and Cheryl Fretz Carlyle, 1978.
25. "All Around Town". *The Buffalo Courier*, 30 Aug. 1890, p. 5.
26. "Life and History of John E. Rebstock, Founder of Crystal Beach". Rebstock, George J. & Helen, and Cheryl Fretz Carlyle, 1978.
27. "Buffalo Men Going South", *Buffalo Evening News*, 31 May, 1889, pg. 2.
28. "Fishing's Fine in Florida". *Buffalo Evening News*, 16 Apr. 1913, p. 14.
29. Personal interview with daughter of Chief William Diamond, 20 Apr. 2021.
30. Walsh, Thomas, "Summer Playground". *Maclean's Magazine*, 1 June 1951. https://archive.macleans.ca/article/1951/06/01/summer-playground, accessed 21 Apr. 2021.
31. "Crystal Beach is Planning Greater Dignity". *Courier Express*, 24 Aug. 1919.

32. "Contracts Let". *Buffalo Evening News*, 22 Apr. 1921.
33. "Crystal Beach has Fire Department". Buffalo newspaper article, 7 May 1913.
34. Personal experience as a Social Services Caseworker in Crystal Beach.
35. Warner, Gene "Van Hall, last owner of Crystal Beach, dies at age 80". buffalonews.com/news/local/van-hall-last-owner-of-crystal-beach-dies-at-age-80/article_75e47b80-18f6-53b6-b0a6-f0f3079eeffa.html. accessed 17 June 2021.
36. Wismer, Jennifer, "From Amusement Thrills to Summertime Chills", Maters Thesis, Queens University, 2001, National Library of Canada, Census of Canada, 1966- Table 9, p. 93. https://central.bac-lac.gc.ca/.item?id=MQ63391&op=pdf&app=Library&oclc_number=1006760740, accessed 22 May 2019.
37. Index of Fire Insurance Plan of Crystal Beach (1927), Crystal Beach, Ont.: digitalarchive.mcmaster.ca, accessed 10 June 2021.
38. "Camp Life". Buffalo Newspaper article, 18 Jul. 1896, www.newspapers.com, accessed 18 June 2021.
39. "Hostess House to be Established at Crystal Beach" Buffalo news article, 2 Jul. 1921.
40. "Young men, women in Scanty Attire Absent". *Niagara Falls Gazette*, 10 July 1953, p. 25.
41. "Life and History of John E. Rebstock, Founder of Crystal Beach". Rebstock, George J. & Helen and Cheryl Fretz Carlyle, 1978.
42. Cy Bell, The Joe Schuster Awards, joeshusterawards.com/hof/bell-cy-1904-197/, accessed 13 June 2021.
43. Personal interview with girl's brother. 6 Mar. 2021.
44. FBI Surveillance Report #124-10346-10370, 22 May 1964, released 14 Nov. 2017, www.archives.gov/files/research/jfk/releases/docid-32316250.pdf, accessed 5 Mar. 2021.
45. Personal interviews with both parties.
46. Personal interview.
47. Wismer, p. 90.

48. "Crystal Beach Dominant Summer Resort". *The Tourist Review,* 7 July 1948, Vol. 1 No. 1.

CHAPTER ONE PHOTOS/IMAGES

John E. Rebstock, founder of Crystal Beach. Photo courtesy Cheryl Fretz Carlyle.

John E. Rebstock's home today on Rebstock Road. Photo by author.

Buffalo Morning Express dateline banner. *Buffalo Morning Express and Illustrated Buffalo Express,* 2 Jul. 1887, pg. 8,

https://www.newspapers.com/image/345038499 downloaded 21 Jul. 2021.

Charles Rano Crystal Beach Announcement, *Buffalo Morning Express and Illustrated Buffalo Express,* 2 Jul. 1887, pg. 8,

https://www.newspapers.com/image/345038499 downloaded 21 Jul. 2021.

Crystal Beach Advertisement, *Buffalo Enquirer,* Aug. 1894.

The Supply House. Photo courtesy Cathy Herbert.

1895 view of Derby Road. Photo courtesy Cheryl Fretz Carlyle.

Hotel Royal, *Fort Erie Local History,* accessed September 6, 2021, http://www.fepl.ca/localhistory/items/show/1775.

Crystal Beach core area map: courtesy John Docker.

Queens Circle dedication stone: Photo by author.

Crystal Beach Boardwalk, 1908. Photo courtesy Clark Family.

1916 Crystal Beach Clown. *Fort Erie Local History,* http://www.fepl.ca/localhistory/items/show/1792, accessed 27 June 2021.

Canadiana leaving Buffalo on her Maiden Voyage, 1910, WNY Heritage Press, PD-US, https://en.wikipedia.org/w/index.php?curid=23644740, accessed 1 May, 2021.

Crystal Beach Arcade Coin, 1947. Photo: Author.

The Comet, Photo by Dale Roddick.

The Midway in Winter, 1911. Photo courtesy Clark Family.

Crystal Beach village letterhead crest. Courtesy Eugene Mallais.

Crystal Beach Volunteer Fire Department, 1960s. Photo courtesy Frank Thornton.

Crystal Beach Amusement Park, 1949. Photo courtesy Cathy Herbert.

Hot Dog Alley 1922: "Crystal Beach, #2," *Fort Erie Local History*, accessed September 10, 2021, http://www.fepl.ca/localhistory/items/show/4870.

Hot Dog Alley 1970s. Photo by Paul Kassay, courtesy Kassay family.

Cronfelt's Loganberry. Photo by Paul Kassay, courtesy Rick Doan.

Sam Aquilina. Photo by Rick Doan, courtesy Cathy Herbert.

The Park in Winter Hibernation. Photo by Dale Roddick.

Skip, the Flagpole Sitter. Photo by Paul Kassay, courtesy Rick Doan.

Johnny Canuck by Leo Bachle. Panel from "Johnny Canuck". Dime Comics, No. 21, June 1945, p. 23. Bell Features Collection, Library and Archives Canada.

1960's Crystal Beach postcard. Photo by Gord Counsell.

John E. Rebstock, founder of Crystal Beach. Photo courtesy Tim Rebstock.

CHAPTER TWO SOURCES

1. Niagara Settler's Land Records, Bertie Township Abstracts. D215 #14185, B182 #11810, sites.google.com/site/niagarasettlers2/bertie-township-abstracts/bertie-map-undated?authuser=0, accessed 27 June 2021.
2. Siler, George "Big Men Fought". *Buffalo Courier Express*, 25 Nov. 1906, p. 37.
3. "The Great Prize Fight". *Sacramento Daily Union*, 3 Sept. 1857.

4. "The Recent Prize Fight". *New York Daily Tribune*, 4 Aug. 1857, p. 5.
5. Siler, George "Big Men Fought". *Buffalo Courier Express*, 25 Nov. 1906, p. 37,
6. "The Great Prize Fight". *Sacramento Daily Union*, 3 Sept. 1857.
7. "The Recent Prize Fight". *New York Daily Tribune*, 4 Aug. 1857, p. 5.
8. "The Great Prize Fight". *Sacramento Daily Union*, 3 Sept. 1857.
9. "The Last of a Famous Prizefighter's Sons". *New York Sun*, 18 June 1884.
10. Asbury, Herbert. *The Gangs of New York: An Informal History of the New York Underworld*. New York: Alfred A. Knopf, 1928. p. 174.
11. "Official Report". *New York Clipper*, 17 Oct. 1857, p. 202
12. "The Last of a Famous Prizefighter's Sons". *New York Sun*, 18 June 1884.
13. "Two Executions". *The New York Times*, 18 Aug. 1866.
14. "The Great Prize Fight". *New York Herald*, 7 Oct. 1959.
15. Ibid.
16. "The Ring". *New York Clipper,* 2 Jan. 1858, p. 290.
17. "Female Prize Fight". *Scranton Republican*, 17 Sept. 1888.
18. "Hattie Leslie Wins". *Buffalo Evening News,* 17 Sept. 1888.

CHAPTER TWO PHOTOS/IMAGES

Point Abino. Photo: Author.

The Great Prizefight between Heenan and Morrisey, Long Point, Ontario, 1858.

Frank Leslie's illustrated newspaper, 30 Oct. 1858, p. 343. www.loc.gov/item/98500131/ retrieved 11 Aug. 2021.

John Camel Heenan. Lithograph, circa 1863.jpeg. Photo by Frederick William Nichols. https://commons.wikimedia.org/w/index.php?searc

h=john+c+heenan&title=Special:MediaSearch&go=Go&type=image, retrieved 7 Mar. 2021.

Hattie Leslie. Photo from National Police Gazette, 1888. From article "Buffalo's Hattie Leslie was first woman's boxing champion", by Thomas Tarapacki, published 23 Sept. 2018. www.buffalorising.com/2018/09/buffalos-hattie-leslie-was-first-womans-boxing-champion/, retrieved 6 May 2021.

CHAPTER THREE SOURCES

1. Thorn, John "Murder and Mayhem Tra-La". *Gotham History blog*, posted 15 June 2015, https://gothamhistory.com/2015/06/15/murder-and-mayhem-tra-la/, accessed 7 Mar. 2021.
2. Ibid.
3. "The Saugerties Bard". *Murder by Gaslight.com*, posted 23 June 2012, https://villagesaugerties.digitaltowpath.org:10064/content/History#Henry%20Backus,%20%22The%20Saugerties%20Bard%22. accessed 8 Mar. 2021.
4. Bala, Rich "Henry Backus, The Saugerties Bard". https://village-saugerties.digitaltowpath.org:10064/content/History#Henry%20Backus,%20%22The%20Saugerties%20Bard%22, accessed 9 May 2021.
5. "The Great Prize Fight in Canada". *Sacramento Daily Union*, 3 Sep. 1857.
6. "The Ring". *New York Clipper*, 2 Jan. 1858, p. 290.
7. "The Pirate Hicks". *New York Herald*, 14 July 1860, p. 3.
8. "Famous American Crime Mysteries". *New York Telegraph*, 6 Dec. 1903, p. 8.
9. "Terrible and Appalling Tragedy". *New York Herald*, 28 Oct. 1858. accessed 10 Mar. 2021.
10. Thorn.

CHAPTER THREE PHOTOS/IMAGES

"Bradley & Rankin's Prize Fight for $1000 a Side." At Point Abino, Canada, August 1, 1857. By Saugerties Bard. Air: Old Virginia. J. Andrews, Printer, 38 Chatham Street, N.Y., Monographic. Online text. <www.loc.gov/item/amss.as101570/>. retrieved 14 Dec. 2014.

Hudson Lunatic Asylum 1841. Hudson Area Library.

"The Saugerties Bard" sketch by John Hughes Kerbert. PD. From *Murder by Gaslight.com*, posted 23 June 2012, https://villagesaugerties.digitaltowpath.org:10064/content/History#Henry%20Backus,%20%22The%20Saugerties%20Bard%22. retrieved 8 Mar. 2021.

"Dead Rabbits' Fight with the Bowery Boys." By Saugerties Bard. Air: Jordan. J. Andrews, Printer, 38 Chatham Street, N.Y., Monographic. Online text. www.loc.gov/item/amss.sb10094a/. retrieved 9 Mar. 2021.

CHAPTER FOUR SOURCES

1. "At Crystal Beach". *Buffalo Courier Express*, 10 Sept. 1910, p. 59.
2. "Crystal Beach Day". *Illustrated Buffalo Express*, 31 Aug. 1902, p. 15.
3. "Relay Team Will Run Against Kolehmainen". *Buffalo Evening News*, 29 Aug. 1913, p. 10.
4. "Buffalo Courier Derby". *Buffalo Courier*, 9 July 1916, p. 71.
5. "George Alesse wins Courier Derby". *Buffalo Courier*, 5 Aug. 1917, p. 71.
6. "Carl Nisita Wins". *Buffalo Courier*, 6 Aug. 1916, p. 72.
7. "Cotton Wins Courier Derby". *Buffalo Courier*, 3 Aug. 1919.
8. "Will Dedicate Stadium at Crystal". *Buffalo Evening News*. 20 May 1920,
9. Alli, Joe "Don Munson is Winner". *Buffalo Courier Express*, 30 June 1946, p. 4-B.
10. "San Romani in Line". *Buffalo Courier Express*, 14 May 1939, p. 8.

11. Marshall, Tabitha "Phil Edwards". www.thecanadianencyclopedia.ca/en/article/phil-edwards, published Sep. 30, 2016. date accessed 3 Apr. 2021.
12. Korzelius, Gene "Eleven New Champions". *Buffalo Evening News*, 29 Aug. 1929, p. 37.
13. "Championships of District". *Buffalo Courier Express*, 12 July 1930, p. 12.
14. "50 Athletes to Vie". *Buffalo Evening News*, 25 July 1930 p. 26.
15. "Weismuller at Crystal Beach". *Buffalo Evening News*, 30 June 1931, p. 33.
16. Ryan, Ray "Peacock Downs Jesse Owens". *Buffalo Courier Express*, 7 July 1935, p. 8.
17. Ibid.
18. Ibid.
19. Ibid.
20. "Age no Barrier to Peacock". *Philadelphia Enquirer*, 3 July 1946, p. 25.
21. Alli, Joe "Beetham Mehl and Peacock Star". *Buffalo Courier Express*, 20 June 1940, p. 19.
22. McKnight, Michael "Faster than the Fastest". published 4 Nov. 2013, *www.si.com/longform/peacock/index.html*, Sports Illustrated Longform, date accessed 3 Apr. 2021.
23. "Cunningham, Venzke". *Buffalo Courier Express*, 20 Aug. 1938, p. 15.
24. Personal interview with George Rebstock, Jr.
25. Potter, Earl "Sketch of Glenn Cunningham". University of Kansas Press Release, 31 May 1933.
26. "10,000 Track Fans Expected". *Buffalo Evening News*, 20 July 1934, p. 24.
27. Hersey, Mark "Cunningham Calls it a Career". University of Kansas Department of History, 20 Apr. 1940, www.kuhistory.com, accessed 21 July 2006.
28. "10,000 Track Fans Expected". *Buffalo Evening News*, 20 July 1934, p. 24.
29. "Falls Man Finds". *Niagara Falls Gazette*, 23 July 1934, p. 15.

30. "Ben Johnson, American Sprinter". https://en.wikipedia.org/wiki/Ben_Johnson_(American_sprinter) accessed 21 May 2021.
31. Alli, Joe "Kansan Beats Venzke". *Buffalo Courier Express*, 21 Aug. 1938, p. 5.
32. "Track Aces Here". *Buffalo Evening News*, 27 Dec. 1939, p. 22.
33. "Olympic Club Entry Lists". *Buffalo Evening News*, 6 June 1938, p. 21.
34. Ranallo, Phil "Fredonia Youth Wins". *Buffalo Courier Express*, 20 June 1948, p. 9-B.
35. Coughlin, Billy "Ellicott District Takes C-E Cup". *Buffalo Courier Express*, 20 June 1950.
36. "Rocky Ending Four Day Tour". *Lockport Union Sun*, 25 Aug. 1962.
37. "Flames Sweep 7400 Seats". *Buffalo Courier Express*, 9 Sept. 1957, p. 1.

CHAPTER FOUR PHOTOS/IMAGES

Crystal Beach Athletic Field. Toronto Star Photograph Archive, Courtesy of Toronto Public Library. www.torontopubliclibrary.ca/digital-archive/, accessed 17 Apr. 2021.

Hans Kolehmainen. *Buffalo Evening News*, 29 Aug. 1913, p. 13.

Crystal Beach athletic field, circa 1910s. Source: Unknown.

The Grandstands at Crystal Beach Stadium. Photo by Paul Kassay, courtesy Rick Doan.

Results of 1925 Courier Derby. *Buffalo Courier Express*, 12 July 1925.

Early track race at Crystal Beach athletic field. Source and date unknown.

Phil Edwards 1928 Olympics. Courtesy Canadian Sports Hall of Fame.

Crystal Beach from an Aeroplane, 1920, Canadian Postcard Company, Wikimedia Commons. https://commons.wikimedia.org/wiki/

File:Crystal Beach Ontario from an Aeroplane (HS85-10-37564).jpg. accessed 7 May, 2021. Public domain.

Jesse Owens and Eulace Peacock in Crystal Beach, 1935. *Buffalo Courier Express*, 7 July 1935.

Jesse Owens at the 1936 Olympics. Official Olympic postcard, Reichssportverlag, Berlin. commons.wikimedia.org licensed under CC BY-SA 4.0. accessed 21 Aug. 2021.

Eulace Peacock winning the 100, Crystal Beach, 1940. *Buffalo Courier Express*, 20 June 1940.

Stadium Ad, Cunningham and Louis: reproduced from *Buffalo Evening News*, 19 Aug.1938.

Glenn Cunningham, 1934. *Buffalo Evening News*, 20 July 1934, p. 24.

Glenn Cunningham at Crystal Beach, 1937. Photo courtesy George R. Rebstock.

Glenn Cunningham at Crystal Beach, 1938. *Buffalo Courier Express*, 21 Aug. 1938.

Gloria Swanson at Crystal Beach Stadium, 1950. *Buffalo Courier Express*, 30 June 1950, p. 24.

Crystal Beach Stadium in flames, 1957. Photo courtesy Cathy Herbert.

Crystal Beach Stadium, south gate, late 1980's. Photo courtesy Cathy Herbert.

CHAPTER FIVE SOURCES

1. "Inquest To Be Held". *Buffalo Courier Express*, 1 June 1938, p. 22.
2. "Teenagers Knife Battle". The Leader Herald, Gloversville and Johnstown, 31 May 1956.
3. "Crystal Beach's Terror". *The Buffalo Express*, 5 Aug. 1895, p. 6.
4. "New Park Police". Newspaper article, unknown publication, 02 June 1949.

5. "Police Chief Beaten". *Buffalo Evening News*, 17 June 1946, p. 1.
6. "Holiday Voyage Ends in Terror". *Utica Observer Dispatch*, 31 May 1956, p. 1.
7. "Crystal Beach Dominant Summer Resort". *The Tourist Review*, 7 July 1948, Vol. 1 No. 1.
8. "Crystal Beach's Terror". *The Buffalo Express*, 5 Aug. 1895, p. 6.
9. "Police Met the Boat". *The Buffalo Express*, 7 Sept. 1897.
10. "Incendiaries at Crystal Beach". *The Buffalo Review*, 29 Aug. 1899, p. 5.
11. Higley, Dahn. O.P.P.: T*he History of the Ontario Provincial Police.* Toronto: The Queens Printer, 1984, p. 94, ISBN 0-7743-8964-8.
12. "Contracts Let". *Buffalo Evening News*, 22 Apr. 1921, p. 20.
13. "The Crystal Beach Situation". *Buffalo Evening News*, 6 July 1951.
14. "Debauchery Tales". *Buffalo Courier Express*, 14 Aug. 1929.
15. "Beach Police Face Ouster". *Buffalo Courier Express*, 1 July 1951, p. 2-B.
16. Kelly, Ed "The Crystal Beach Situation". *Buffalo Evening News*, 6 July 1951.
17. "Tales of Merry Doings". *Buffalo Courier Express*, 15 June 1925, p. 3.
18. "Hold Three on Shooting Charge". *Niagara Falls Gazette*, 22 June 1927, p. 10.
19. "Crystal Beach Police Chief". *Buffalo Courier Express*, 21 June 1929, p. 1.
20. "Crystal Beach Police" *Buffalo Evening News*, 5 Sept. 1929.
21. "Ontario Police Arrest Americans". *Buffalo Evening News*, 24 June 1929, p. 1.
22. "Orders Inquiry". *Buffalo Courier Express*, 14 Aug. 1929, p. 24.
23. "Ridgeway", *Buffalo Evening News* 28 Oct. 1913, p. 8.
24. "Crowe Made Chief". *Buffalo Evening News*, 24 Apr. 1925.
25. "Port Colborne Cops Clear". *Buffalo Evening News*, 21 Dec. 1925.

26. Johnson, Brian, "Positively Gleeful". *Maclean's Magazine*, 27 May 2010, www.macleans.ca/culture/positively-gleeful/, accessed 6 June 2021.
27. "$1,000,000 Port Colborne Syndicate Exports Ten Carloads of Liquor for U. S. Holiday Enjoyment". *Buffalo Courier Express*, 5 Dec. 1926, p. 2.
28. "Canada Hits at Rum Runners". *Buffalo Courier Express*, 20 May 1928.
29. "Change in Ontario Dry Act". *Buffalo Evening News*, 12 Aug. 1926,
30. "Business Slow". *Buffalo Courier Express*, 16 Sep. 1928, p. 8.
31. "Distillery at Port Colborne Sold". Niagara Falls Gazette, 6 Mar. 1929, p. 14.
32. "Highland Scotch Distillers." Port Colborne Historical and Marine Museum Records.
33. "Port Colborne Cop Clear". *Buffalo Evening News*, 21 Dec. 1925.
34. "Frank Reavley". *Niagara Falls Gazette*, 23 Feb. 1926, p. 10.
35. "Ridgeway Ontario". *Buffalo Evening News*, 3 Aug. 1929, p. 4.
36. "Crystal Beach Ontario". *Buffalo Evening News*, 24 June 1932, p. 29.
37. "Crystal Beach Man". *Buffalo Courier Express*, 5 July 1933, p. 18.
38. "Doubt is Expressed". *Buffalo Evening News*, 5 Oct. 1934, p. 8.
39. "Advises Buffalo Man". *Buffalo Courier Express*, 11 July 1934, p. 11.
40. "CNR Brakeman Fatally Injured". *Niagara Falls Gazette*, 24 June 1944, p. 5.
41. "Slot Machines Ordered". *Buffalo Courier Express*, 4 July 1936, p. 9.
42. "Chef for Buffalo Veteran". *Buffalo Evening News*, 19 Oct. 1931.
43. "Judge to Study Evidence". *Buffalo Courier Express*, 7 Dec. 1946, p. 10.
44. "Resigned Official". *Buffalo Evening News*, 14 Aug. 1946.
45. "Judge to Study Evidence". *Buffalo Courier Express*, 7 Dec. 1946, p. 10.

46. "Judge Reverses Ruling". *Buffalo Courier Express*, 24 Apr. 1947, p. 25.
47. "Resigned Official". *Buffalo Evening News*, 14 Aug. 1946.
48. "Fight Indicated". *Buffalo Evening News*, 19 Feb. 1949, p. 1.
49. Ibid.
50. "Crystal Beach Council". *Buffalo Courier Express*, 4 July 1950.
51. "5 Day Suspension". *Buffalo Evening News*, 22 Feb. 1949.
52. "Crystal Beach Council". *Buffalo Courier Express*, 5 July 1950.
53. "Doctor Tells of Examining Attack Victim". *Buffalo Courier Express*, 27 Sept. 1949, p. 8.
54. "Buffalo Youth Gets Three Years". *Niagara Falls Gazette*, 30 Sept. 1949, p. 25.
55. "Conviction of Buffalo Youth Quashed". *Niagara Falls Gazette*, 17 Dec. 1949, p.14.
56. "U.S. Narcotics Agents Seek More Suspects". *Buffalo Evening News*, 3 Oct. 1952, p. 36.
57. "Fourth Youth Sought". *Buffalo Evening News*, 4 Nov. 1946, p. 1.
58. "Boyd and Hawkins Sentenced to Life". *Buffalo Evening News*, 28 Feb. 1947, p. 35.
59. "Three Canadians Seized". *Buffalo Evening News*, 26 Jan. 1950.
60. "Police Chief Befriends Accused". *Buffalo Courier Express*, 8 Aug. 1947.
61. "Crystal Beach Council Accepts Resignation". *Buffalo Courier Express*, 4 July 1950.
62. "Crystal Beach Council". *Buffalo Evening News*, 5 July 1951.
63. "Magistrate Sentences". *Bowmanville Canadian Statesman*, 21 Aug. 1963, p. 13. http://images.ourontario.ca/Partners/ClaPL/CLaPL002715361pf_0014.pdf, accessed 15 Mar. 2021
64. "Reeve Ousts Police". *Buffalo Courier Express*, 4 July 1951.
65. "The Crystal Beach Situation". *Buffalo Evening News*, 6 July 1951.
66. "Beach Police Face Ouster". *Buffalo Courier Express*, 1 July 1951, p. 2-B.
67. Ibid.
68. "Beach Murder". *Buffalo Courier Express*, 20 Sept. 1951 p. 27.

69. Ibid.
70. "Slashed Clothing". *Buffalo Evening News*, 19 Sept. 1951.
71. "1st Degree Murder Count". *Buffalo Evening News*, 18 June 1951.
72. "Wife Slayer". *Buffalo Courier Express*, 18 June 1951, p. 1.
73. Ibid.
74. "Beach Police". *Buffalo Courier Express*, 1 July 1951, p. 2-B.
75. Newspaper Article, Unknown Publication, Sept. 1951.
76. "Man Kills Self". *Buffalo Courier Express*, 25 Oct. 1953.
77. "Crystal Beach Council". *Buffalo Evening News*, 5 July 1951.
78. "Fire Chief is Reinstated". *Buffalo Evening News*, 11 July 1951.
79. "Beach Council". *Buffalo Courier Express*, 24 July 1951, p. 15.
80. "Two Suspended". *Buffalo Evening News*, 3 July 1951, p. 19.
81. Kustas, Lou "Provincial Police May Be Employed". Buffalo Evening News, 24 Jul. 1951.
82. "Two Swift Raids". *Buffalo Evening News*, 14 July 1951, p. 1.
83. "Two Fined $500". *Olean Times Herald*, 26 July 1951, p. 1.
84. "Crystal Beach gets O.P.P. Force". *Niagara Falls Gazette*, 3 Oct. 1951, p. 38.
85. "Police Term Shooting an Accident". *Fort Erie Times Review*, 4 May 1977.
86. Personal interviews of confidential sources.
87. "Woman Charged in Slaying". *Buffalo Evening News*, 24 Aug. 2001.
88. "Man Guilty of Second-Degree Murder". Niagara This Week, 24 Jan. 2008. www.niagarathisweek.com/news-story/3292184-man-guilty-of-second-degree-murder-in-crystal-beach/, accessed 31 May 2021.
89. Wismer, Jennifer, "From Amusement Thrills to Summertime Chills", Maters Thesis, Queens University, 2001, National library of Canada, Census of Canada, 1966- Table 9, p. 93. https://central.bac- lac.gc.ca/.item?id=MQ63391&op=pdf&app=Library&oclc_number=1006760740, accessed 22 May 2019.

90. Census Profile, 2016 Census, www12.statcan.gc.ca/census-recensement/2016/, accessed 31 May 2021.

CHAPTER FIVE PHOTOS/IMAGES

Crystal Beach constable's badge: Courtesy Mark Chernish.

Chief Frank Reavley: Sidney Morris Jr. collection, courtesy David Radley.

Chief Floyd Garrard, with retired chief Frank Reavley: Photo: Sidney Morris Jr. collection.

Chief Percy Mark, centre, and Crystal Beach P.D. circa 1946: Courtesy Frank Thornton.

Bernard Kitney and Bowmanville Police Force, circa 1960: Courtesy Myno Van Dyke.

Chateau Flamingo, scene of the Bassett murder: Courtesy Shawn Moore.

Constable John Sandel arresting Fifi the Clown, 1950: Courtesy Gary Sandel.

Crystal Beach O.P.P. Detachment sign: Author.

Provincial Constable Jerry Deheus: Courtesy Jerry Deheus.

CHAPTER SIX SOURCES

1. "Bestow Another Decoration". *Buffalo Courier Express*, 6 July 1925, p. 14.
2. Batchelor, Peter, and *Christopher Matson*. VCs of the First World War - The Western Front 1915. *Sutton Publishing, Cheltenham, U.K. 1998*, p. 3, ISBN 0-7509-1980-9.
3. *Batchelor & Matson*, p. 2.
4. Batchelor & Matson, p. 1.
5. *Batchelor & Matson*, p. 2.

6. "Weapons of War- Machine Guns". www.firstworldwar.com/weaponry/machineguns.htm, accessed 12 June 2021.
7. *Batchelor & Matson*, p. 2.
8. *Ibid.*
9. Fourth Supplement to The London Gazette of 16 February 1915. 18 February 1915, Numb. 29074, p. 1700, https://vcgca.org/our-people/profile/218/Michael-O-LEARY, accessed 15 May 2021.
10. Batchelor & Matson, p. 3.
11. Sir Arthur Conan Doyle, *"Michael O'Leary VC"*, Ballingeary & Inchigeela Historical Society, www.ballingearyhs.com/journal2001/michael_oleary.html, accessed 1 Apr, 2021.
12. *Batchelor & Matson.*
13. "Applies for Position". *Niagara Falls Gazette,* 21 Apr. 1926, p.12.
14. Higley, p. 15.
15. "O'Leary Arrested Again". *New York Times,* 6 Sept. 1925, p. 2.
16. "War Hero New Police Chief". *Watertown Daily Standard,* 12 Sept. 1925, p. 12.
17. "O'Leary Goes Back to Jail". *Buffalo Courier Express,* 19 Sept. 1925, p. 3.
18. Ibid.
19. "O'Leary Arrested Again". *New York Times,* 6 Sept. 1925, p. 2.
20. Ibid.
21. "O'Leary Goes Back to Jail". *Buffalo Courier Express,* 19 Sept. 1925, p. 3.
22. "Another Man is Sought". *Buffalo Evening New*s, 8 Sept. 1925.
23. "Will Investigate flow of Liquor". *Buffalo Courier Express,* 9 Sept. 1925 p. 14.
24. Johnson, Brian "Positively Gleeful". *Maclean's Magazine,* 27 May 2010, www.macleans.ca/culture/positively-gleeful/, accessed 6 June 2021.
25. "Rum Chasers". *Buffalo Evening News,* 2 July 1925, p. 30.
26. "Uses Billy to Subdue Policeman". *Buffalo Courier Express,* 4 July 1928, p. 15.

27. "No Barriers in Sight". *Buffalo Courier Express*, 28 July 1928, p. 4.
28. "Beach Police Deny". *Buffalo Courier Express*, 20 Aug. 1928, p. 11.
29. "Applies for Position". *Niagara Falls Gazette*, 21 Apr. 1926, p.12.
30. Batchelor & Matson, p. 5.
31. "Michael O'Leary, V.C.". *Buffalo Evening News*, 11 Oct. 1929.
32. Batchelor & Matson, p. 5.

CHAPTER SIX PHOTOS/IMAGES

Chief of Police Michael John O'Leary, www.memorialstovalour.co.uk/vc569.html, accessed 15 Mar. 2021.

German Machine Gun Crew,

period5team1.weebly.com/machine-guns.html, accessed 12 June 2021.

German Maschinengewehr MG-08. Photo: en.wikipedia.org.jpg, PD, accessed 12 June 2021.

An Irish hero! ... Sergeant Michael O'Leary, V.C... Join an Irish regiment to-day / David Allen & Sons Ltd., 40, Great Brunswick St., Dublin. Great Britain Ireland, 1915. [S.l.: s.n] Photograph. https://www.loc.gov/item/2003668492/.

Michael O'Leary's medals on display. Photo by Thomas Stewart, www.vconline.org.uk/michael-j-oleary-vc/4587805344, accessed 18 Mar. 2021.

Michael O'Leary Memorial, RCMP Training Depot, Regina Saskatchewan. Photo: Dan Pooler.

CHAPTER SEVEN SOURCES

1. "Life and History of John E. Rebstock, Founder of Crystal Beach". Rebstock, George J. & Helen, and Cheryl Fretz Carlyle, 1978.
2. U.S. Census, Buffalo, Erie County, New York, 1900.
3. U.S. Census, Buffalo, Erie County, New York, 1905.
4. Quebec Census, Saint-Rémi, Laprairie & Napierville, QC, 1901.
5. "Omer Hébert's Girly Jazzy Review". *Wayland New York Register*, 9 Sept. 1920.
6. "Melody Mirth and Music". *Cohocton N.Y. Valley Times*, 22 Sept. 1920.
7. "Omer Hébert's Girly Jazzy Review" *The Wayland Register*, 9 Sep. 1920.
8. "Saxophone Sextet Feature". *Hornell Evening Tribune Times*, 22 Sep. 1920.
9. "Plattsburg Theater Today". *Plattsburgh Daily Press*, 29 Jun. 1920.
10. "Mrs. Hébert's Rites Will Be Held Today". Ruth Hébert Obituary, *Buffalo Courier Express*, 2 Nov. 1952.
11. E-mail from Carolyn Klotzbach-Russel, "Ruth Hébert", received by G. Pooler, 3 Mar. 2021.
12. Omer Hébert's military induction record.
13. "Dancer's Legacy for Playground". Canadian Press, Nov. 1952.
14. U.S. Census, Buffalo, Erie County, New York, 1900.
15. U.S. Census, Buffalo, Erie County, New York, 1905.
16. "Kinsmen Pledge We Won't Sell". *Fort Erie Times-Review*, Apr. 1972.
17. "20-year-old dream by Kinsmen got a boost from Lions". *Fort Erie Times-Review*, 25 Nov. 1974.
18. "Solidly Booked Already". *Fort Erie Times Review*, 25 Nov. 1974.

CHAPTER SEVEN PHOTOS/IMAGES:

Omer, Ruth, Burt Peck: *Hornell Evening Tribune-Times*, 24 Sep. 1920, p. 9.

The Hébert Hotel, 1930s. Photo: Courtesy Shawn Moore.

Jimmy Iezzi, Manager, Hébert's Hotel. Photo: courtesy Larry and Elaine Culling.

"Dancer's Legacy for Playground". Canadian Press, 1952.

Ruth Hébert, *The Buffalo Courier*, 12 Oct. 1919.

CHAPTER EIGHT PHOTOS/IMAGES

Crystal Beach B.I.A. welcome sign. Photo: Author.

The Comet, after the park's closing. 1989. Photo: Cathy Herbert.

The Canadiana propeller and capstan. Photo: Author.

December 24, 1989. Three months after closing. Photo: Cathy Herbert.

Where the Crystal Beach Amusement Park once stood. Photo: Author.

Crystal Beach Amusement Park commemorative sign. Photo: Author.

Lightning Source UK Ltd.
Milton Keynes UK
UKHW011148040322
399574UK00001B/114